SPECIAL LOVE / SPECIAL SEX

Utopianism and Communitarianism
Lyman Tower Sargent and Gregory Claeys
Series Editors

The John Ben Snow Prize

This prize is given annually by the Press for an original manuscript of nonfiction dealing with some aspect of New York State.

Recipients:

1978

Warrior in Two Camps

William H. Armstrong

1979

Black Education in New York State

Carleton Mabee

1980

Landmarks of Otsego County

Diantha Dow Schull

1981

Joseph Brant, 1743–1807

Isabel Thompson Kelsay

1982

Upstate Travels

Roger Haydon

1983

Gustav Stickley, the Craftsman

Mary Ann Smith

1984

Images of Rural Life

DeWitt Historical Society of Tompkins County

Marietta Holley

Kate H. Winter

1985

Upstate Literature

Frank Bergmann, editor et al.

1986

Proud Patriot

Don R. Gerlach

1987

Old-Time Music Makers of New York State

Simon J. Bronner

1988

No prize given

1989

Landmarks of Oswego County

Judith Wellmann

1990

Clear Pond

Roger Mitchell

1991

Women's Humor in the Age of Gentility

Linda A. Morris

1992

Make a Way Somehow

Kathryn Grover

1993

No prize given

1994

Special Love/Special Sex

Robert S. Fogarty, editor

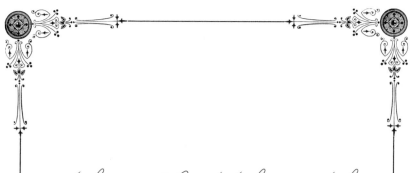

Special Love / Special Sex

AN ONEIDA COMMUNITY DIARY

Edited by

ROBERT S. FOGARTY

Syracuse University Press

First Edition 1994

94 95 96 97 98 99   6 5 4 3 2 1

This book is published with the assistance of the John Ben Snow Foundation.

The paper used in this publication meets the minimum requirements of American National Standard for Information Sciences—Permanence of Paper for Printed Library Materials, ANSI Z39.48-1984. ∞™

Library of Congress Cataloging-in-Publication Data
Hawley, Victor.
    Special love/special sex : an Oneida Community diary / edited by
Robert S. Fogarty.
        p.   cm. — (Utopianism and communitarianism)
    Victor Hawley's complete diary turned into a dialogue between the
text and editor.
    Includes bibliographical references and index.
    ISBN 0-8156-0286-3. — ISBN 0-8156-2622-3 (pbk.)
    1. Oneida Community. 2. Hawley, Victor—Diaries. 3. Free love—
United States—History—19th century. I. Fogarty, Robert S.
II. Title. III. Series.
HX656.O5H39 1994
306.73'5—dc20   94-7448

Manufactured in the United States of America

For Katherine

Robert S. Fogarty is Professor of History at Antioch College and editor of *The Antioch Review*. A leading authority on American communes, his most recent book is *All Things New: American Communes and Utopian Movements, 1860–1914*. He has been a Visiting Fellow at All Souls, Oxford, and the New York University Institute for the Humanities.

*Y*ou know Schopenhauer says that everything is constructed around the dominant seventh; we cannot be happy except as we pass from unhappiness. The discords in the life of the community—meaning the suffering caused by strict regulations—were so arranged that there was more of a chance of resolution into a chord of happiness than in monogamic discords and consequently, in my opinion, a higher average happiness, sexually.

—Theodore Noyes, 1892

Contents

Illustrations

Preface

𝒯he main source for this book, the "Special Love/Special Sex," came to me by the most serendipitous route. My interest in the Oneida Community has been a long-standing one, beginning when I spent six months in the early 1960s working at the Lena R. Arents Rare Book Room at Syracuse University reading through some forty years of periodicals produced by John H. Noyes and his associates. At that time primary sources about the colony were few, and scholars relied on printed collections compiled by descendants and on the periodical materials gathered by Lester G. Wells into the Arents Collection in the early 1960s. Wells, then curator of the collection and now deceased, had provided me with a personal introduction to some community descendants.

I thought myself fortunate to have Wells as a guide and to meet some Oneida descendants who were willing to talk about their memories of the community. Eventually, I wrote a dissertation on the Oneida Community. But I knew full well that a genuine history could never be written without additional source material, particularly about the community's internal life and, most notably, about its sexual life. During the 1970s I published articles on the community, edited an edition of their community newsletter, *The Daily Journal,* encouraged other scholars to use the Oneida material within a comparative context, and saw Maren Lockwood Carden gain access to certain colony records for her study. The field of communal history is a large one, and there were numerous projects around to engage any scholar; so I kept busy with several projects leading to my *Dictionary of American Communal History* (1980), *The Righteous Remnant: The House of David* (1981), and *All Things New: American Communes and Utopian Movements, 1860–1914* (1990). Yet Oneida remained an engrossing topic for me, and a series of chance encounters led me to a remarkible document about Oneida that served to illuminate certain dark corners of its history and all that the colony represents in our social history.

The first encounter came in 1980, after a session of the Organization of American Historians on "Sexuality and Ante-Bellum Communities" that I chaired. At the end of the session Robert Lehman, of Miami University, asked if I would like to see an Oneida diary that his brother-in-law had in his possession. Knowing that there were virtually no diaries outside of community hands, I expressed great interest. Almost two years lapsed between that encounter and a phone call to my office from Prof. Lehman, who asked if I still wanted to see the diary. The answer was "Yes, of course!" but at that point I was still immersed in a study of post–Civil War communities. Shortly thereafter, a fair transcript of the diary, done in painstaking fashion by Melville Hawley of Smyrna, Florida, arrived. He had carefully gone through the faded entries of the diary (he had received it from his sister, Martha Hawley Straub) of his distant relative, Victor Hawley, and he had produced an accurate rendering of it from the script; yet there were numerous omissions, noted by the letters *SH*, where parts of the diary had been kept in shorthand. Hawley had no luck in deciphering the notations, and Pitman experts in the United States could offer no help.

At this point I knew that I had to see the original diary, then held by Richard McCartney, a relative of Hawley living north of Syracuse, New York. The following fall, while I was in Binghamton, I called McCartney to arrange a meeting so that I could see the diaries. I suggested that we meet at the Everson Museum and he countered with a better suggestion—that we meet at Heid's, a famous local hot dog stand. We met in the parking lot of Heid's on a lovely fall day, and

McCartney took from his pocket two slim volumes, (2½″ x
3½″) bound in leather and held together by a rubber band.
Respectful of his own genealogy because of his Mormon faith,
Richard McCartney had no qualms about sharing the diaries
with anyone interested in family history. In an outstanding
act of generosity he said that I could not only see the diaries,
but take them with me, knowing that I was intending to
travel abroad. The sojourn turned out to be a fortunate one
because during my stay in London I contacted the Pitman organization, which gave me a slim lead in the form of a name
of someone who might be able to help decipher the shorthand
entries.

The name was that of Mabel Charlesworth of Oxfordshire,
who, if she had lived in Japan, would have the status of a
national treasure; however, in Britain her unusual talent
brought her little fame and even less money. She agreed to
attempt to decipher the shorthand notations, and her painstaking work convinced me that the diary was not just unusual, but unique. On the face of it, being able to comprehend
shorthand sounds like a modest skill until you are confronted
with a page of dimly noted marks that may or may not form a
coherent pattern. The pattern in the Hawley diary was not
Pitman, as we learned, but an American variant, Munson, in-
vented in the 1860s by a New York court stenographer and
subsequently used at Oneida. Munson is no longer used, and
its marking pattern varies considerably from that of the
Pitman script. It is, in fact, a dead language, and Mabel
Charlesworth is, I suspect, its only student.

She is more than a student of shorthand; she is an inter-
preter of the line, the dash, the dot, the incomplete stroke—
the stylistic eccentricities that distinguish one hand from another. She struggled with Victor Hawley's Munson notations
(many in fading pencil), and then one evening we pieced out
the last difficult and remaining shorthand sections of the diary. Like all diarists, Hawley had kept his record secret and
yet resorted to shorthand to bury deeper certain facts: such as
the times when he and Mary Jones had "connection" (a eu-
phemism for sexual intercourse); such as his despair over the
possibility of having a child with her; such as his doubts

about community life. Only about 10 percent of the diary was kept in Munson, and much of that appears in the first few months. The shorthand notations were crucial to the two-year record he kept of his struggle with himself and with the elders at Oneida in his ongoing effort to find a solution to his love needs. Victor Hawley's diary represents the deepest conflicts that Oneida faced, the most repressed of its urges, and in Hawley's script (sometimes coded) we can see the layered life of a community.

With the opening of the Oneida Community Collection in the Arents Rare Book Room at Syracuse University, in 1991, certain facts and facets of the diary could be further explored. Theodore Noyes's own perspective on the stirpiculture experiment became available to all researchers, and John H. Noyes's plan for the future of the community (written while he was in exile in Canada) became known. Maren Lockwood had access to this material for her 1969 study *Oneida: Utopian Community to Modern Corporation,* but she chose to paraphrase those documents rather than to quote them directly and downplayed the explosive effect that sexual politics played within the community. In addition, I examined other diaries within the Oneida Community Collection and in the Nash Collection at Stanford University. Victor Hawley's diary—published here in full—is, by far, the most illuminating document about the Oneida Community to emerge in the last thirty years.

Rather than simply present the diary in annotated form, I have decided to present it as a dialogue between the text and myself. After two initial interpretive chapters, the diary is presented in four separate sections that break at natural turning points. These sections are introduced by my own commentary for each section, which constitutes both a narrative of the events and an interpretation. These sections mirror my own continuous effort to comprehend and understand the life of the community through the eyes and hidden words of one participant in this grand social experiment called the Oneida Community. "Special Sex/Special Love" was once private and seen only by community descendants and is now—for the first time—public. Beyond that documentary value, it is story about anguish and hope and the ways in which men and women saw and confronted one another in a remarkable community family of three hundred in Madison County, New York.

Thus, with the help of Mabel Charlesworth, Richard McCartney, Melville Hawley, Martha Hawley Straub, and Robert Lehman the diary became whole. Lord Poonsby, the famous historian of English diaries, said that "no editor could be trusted not to spoil a diary," according to Thomas Mallon's *A Book of One's Own: People and Their Diaries*. What I have tried to do is to bring this diary to life, to give it flesh in its spare sections, to let it speak in its own voice whenever possible, and to let the story of Victor Hawley and Mary Jones emerge.

For, despite all the sensational and stunning material in the diary it is, at base, a love story about two people and their desire to have a baby. A simple enough story except that it occurs within the Oneida Community and represents unsanctified love in the eyes of the elders. This personal diary written during 1876 and 1877 deals with love, aggression, conflict, and jealousy; it is also a story about the conflict between private desire and public good.

Robert S. Fogarty

Yellow Springs, Ohio
February 1994

Acknowledgments

his book had its origins in a suggestion made during the early years of my graduate study by Professor Allen Du-Pont Breck that I look at the Oneida Community. Breck was both a medievalist and a scholar of American religions and was an inspiration to anyone interested in topics that fell outside a conventional range. Sections of my dissertation subsequently appeared in *The New England Quarterly,* in *Labor History,* and in an introduction to *The O.C. Daily,* and appear here in altered form.

Over the years several scholars have enriched my appreciation of Oneida, most notably my student, Lawrence Foster, whose close reading of religious texts has contributed greatly to my own understanding. Other scholars, like Michael Barkun and Lyman Tower Sargent, have, by their own work, added immesureably to my understanding of the utopian tradition. This diary has accompanied me to several universities, and within their walls I was able to reflect on the meaning of community. At the Johns Hopkins Center for American and Chinese Studies I began to understand another dimension of family planning and its impact on a society, and at All Souls College, Oxford, I realized the pleasures of private space and scholarly study.

Funds for travel to collections have been provided by the Faculty Fund of Antioch College. Librarians in the Manuscript Collections at Stanford University helped me through the Nash Family Papers, and the staff of the Arents Rare

Book Room at the Syracuse University Library have, over the years, answered queries. Under the leadership of the late Lester G. Wells, and now that of Mark Weimer, the Oneida Community Collection has flourished. Each was helpful at every turn. At the Mansion House Gail Doering provided valuable assistance with the photographic collection, and Richard Kathmann was a gracious host. The Hawley family—particularly Mel Hawley of Smyrna Beach, Florida, and Martha Straub Hawley of Los Angeles—generously provided diary material. Mel Hawley's work in first transcribing the diary set the stage for this book, and the late Richard McCartney's offer to let me see the original material made it all possible. I want to acknowledge the administrative staff suport of two assistants, Gerda Oldham and Michelle Giguere, and the help of three student assistants, Jami Hoffman, David Ramm, and Shannon Nunnally Cates. In addition to her staff work Michelle Giguere was responsible for photographing diary material included in this volume. Finally, I want to thank Katherine Kadish, who always knew that this love story was more than a mere "diary" and who encouraged me to try and turn it into something more than another scholarly project. To her this book is dedicated.

Textual Note

$\mathscr{V}$ictor Hawley's two small (2½″ x 3½″) diaries were written in both pen and pencil and contain both longhand and Munson shorthand notations. The space allotted for a daily entry he often filled to the margins of a page, producing a cramped page. At the top of a page (above the printed month, day, year) he often indicated how many hours he worked in the dentist's office, or some other place at Oneida. At the end of each diary there was a "Memoranda" section, which he used to indicate purchases and other cash transactions. These sections have been included.

Although he had a relatively clear hand, Hawley had his idiosyncrasies. For example, his punctuation and capitalization were erratic, and his shorthand notations were often ambiguous about such matters, with some entered in pencil that have faded after a hundred and twenty years. In addition, he was in the habit of breaking words such as those that began with *to* with a space—*to night, to morrow*. He did the same with *al most* and with *tho ught*. In all cases I have erred on the side of readability (joining the parts in these cases) while trying to maintain his own abrupt style. There has been no attempt to render the diary in facsimile form, but there have been no deletions or significant emendations to the text. When, for example, he crossed out a line, or placed hatch marks over a section, that material has remained with appropriate markings. No attempt has been made to indicate errors in spelling or punctuation (for example, sometimes a diary

xxi

entry ends with a period, at other times there is no mark), but
I have tried to allow a reader to follow his actions and state of
mind in the text. For this book it is not the letter of the text
that is most important; it is the diarist's rendering of important events and feelings, however ill put. These diary entries
are more jottings than composed entries.

At certain points it was impossible to interpret the shorthand entries, and a bracketed [SH] has been used at those
places. In a few entries there have been erasures or conspic-
uous gaps in the text, and they have been noted.

SPECIAL LOVE / SPECIAL SEX

Complex Marriage Hymn
by T. L. Pitt

(To the tune of "Jesus I My Cross Have Taken")

*T*he first two verses were sung by the choir on stage at the Mansion House on behalf of new members at the close of the ceremony of admission. The last two verses were sung in response to the choir by the whole congregation, standing.

> Complex husband I espouse thee,
> Sons of Christ and Church of God;
> To obey and cherish ever,
> Love thy scepter, trust thy rod.

> Husband art thou of my choosing,
> Dearer far than all beside,
> Other bonds from me now loosing,
> Here with thee will I abide.

> Spouse that comest, asking blessing,
> Welcome to our hearts and home;
> We and ours are God's possession—
> Christ to wed us bids thee come.

> We will love thee as thou lovest
> Him, the truth, and faithful prove,
> Working for the inner kingdom,
> Living for the heaven of love.

 **CHAPTER ONE**

Oneida
One Home, One Family Relation

> *In the course of the next year at Andover I*
> *had a revelation in my heart that I myself*
> *was going to bring heaven and earth to-*
> *gether—that it was my job.*
> —John H. Noyes,
> "Kingdom of Heaven" (1866)

*O*f all the utopian colonies the Oneida Community (1848–1880) has had the greatest scrutiny and commentary, with historians, psychologists, philosophers, sexologists, and community organizers all having had a turn at understanding this varied and successful experiment in "Bible Communism," as community members called it.

Oneida is studied so intensively because both its history and the role played by its founder and leader, John H. Noyes, are central to the utopian tradition in America. That tradition has been varied and long-lived. Oneida stands midway between the eighteenth-century Shakers, with their intense religious concerns and their withdrawal from the world, and the twentieth-century socialist utopians who hoped to reform the world by cooperative example and political persuasion. Oneida was both religious and secular, in the world and apart from it, a success and a failure. According to Alexander Kent (who surveyed cooperative communities at the turn of the century) it was, he thought, the "one distinctively American community which has claimed for itself a religious base and only one of two American communities which have achieved financial success." Harold Bloom, in *The American Religion: The Emergence of the Post-Christian Nation* (New York, 1992), believes that Oneida does not "trouble our imaginations enough" and sees Noyes as a failed "Gnostic libertine." Beyond that characterization, there is little doubt that Oneida was one of the most complex small groups ever formed. Its origins, its theology, its leadership, its sexual practices, its social arrangements, its economic bases, its dramatic experimental eugenics plan, and its volatile breakup are all large subjects in and of themselves.

Oneida was not merely another "utopian" experiment: it had more than a generational life; it was well known (between 1862 and 1867 it had over forty-five thousand visitors); its goods were sold from New York to California, and in its declining years it developed the now famous Oneida silver plate. Yet there were problems: tensions existed between individual needs and community goals, and there was growing generational conflict. For example, Noyes's own son, Victor, fled the community at one point, sought the help of the reformer and philanthropist Gerrit Smith, and eventually spent some time at the Utica Asylum. The community attributed the sources of his problem to his masturbating, to his reading certain corrupting books (like Goethe's *The Apprenticeship of Wilhelm Meister*), and to his belief that he was the first offspring of the complex marriage system inaugurated at Putney, Vermont, in the 1840s, thus granting him a special place in the community. Throughout its history, however, Oneida did confront numerous significant issues: family planning, child care, women's rights, adult education, job diversification, and the problem of maintaining the communal "family" that had replaced the nuclear family.

To understand John H. Noyes, is, in large measure, to understand Oneida and its formative years. Noyes was a descendant of New England Puritans and so proud of his lineage that he wrote in his spiritual autobiography: "The Puritans had practically identified themselves with the irrepressible

principle lying at the foundation of all success-faith in God."
He was born into a respectable, middle-class family at Brattle-
boro, Vermont, in 1811, and although Noyes's father, a one-term
Congressman and a merchant, was not particularly concerned
about religion, Noyes's mother constantly worried about
the spiritual and moral welfare of the children. At age fifteen young Noyes entered Dartmouth, his father's alma
mater, rather than Yale because it "would be a better place
for his morals," but at Dartmouth his problems were not particularly theological but rather social, since he was plagued
by a sense of insecurity and bashfulness in dealing with
women.

After graduating from Dartmouth, he worked briefly in a
law office; however, in September 1831 he attended a revival
meeting at Putney, Vermont, that transformed his life and
turned him towards the Andover Theological Seminary, hoping to live in the "revival spirit" and to be a "young convert"
forever. Leaving Andover in 1832, he continued his studies at
Yale, where he fell under the influence of the liberal theo-
logian Nathaniel Taylor, whose motto was Follow the Truth If
It Carries You Over Niagara. At this point Noyes identified
himself as an ardent Perfectionist seeking "security from sin"
and a heightened spiritual life, became involved with the
New Haven Anti-Slavery Society, and was embroiled in a
public controversy over two of his sermons. These heretical
sermons were the first of a series of events that led to the
revocation of his preaching license by the Yale Divinity
School in 1834.

Between 1834 and 1843 "young man" Noyes struggled to
find a balance between "self" and "society," between the demands of faith and reason, of theology and prophecy, of the
head and the heart. During this period Noyes emerged as a
public and often controversial figure, particularly when he began to publish his own religious periodical, *The Witness*.
Later, he would write that many of the members at Oneida
"had been brought into the faith either directly or indirectly
by the paper published at New Haven." Throughout his career Noyes sought to publicize both his own personal religious
beliefs and more general reform news in his journals. With

the publication of what later became known as the "Battle-Axe Letter" Noyes's views on free love became known for the first time, and there was an immediate outcry against them; yet he remained undaunted and continued to proselytize for a Perfectionist reform position. For example, when he met William Lloyd Garrison and James Whittier for the first time, he attempted to convert them to that position immediately. In 1838 he married an older woman, Harriet Holton, after being spurned by another, younger woman, Abigail Merwin. Up to this point Noyes was working within a contemporary intellectual and social tradition that included revivalism, sinless Perfectionism, and tract publication. He was a radical within those traditions but had yet to move towards a position that urged and justified community property and "Bible Communism," but the seeds of that justification were to be found in the troubled period surrounding the Panic of 1837. In 1838 Noyes was in flux—like so many other reformers who were tossed about by the religious, social, and economic forces of the period—and seeking to find an appropriate vehicle for both his own personal salvation and social salvation for American society.

During the late 1830s and early 1840s Noyes formed in Vermont the "Putney Society of Believers," a loose confederation of families who lived in common under his leadership, and he published a periodical, *The Perfectionist and Theocratic Watchman*. Noyes's plans included the establishment of a "Universal Manual Labor School" that would combine work and intellectual pursuits (for both men and women) that would lead to the founding of a theological seminary for Perfectionist believers. During this period his wife bore several stillborn children, and her pain and suffering forced him to think about sexual issues and women's role in society. In 1846 the Putney group began to practice, according to Noyes, "complex marriage," which others called "free love." According to Noyes the "kingdom of heaven" had arrived, and sexual exclusiveness was abandoned in favor of community property within the Putney Society of Believers. At this point Noyes began to join both economic and sexual questions in a radical fashion and urged the transformation of society based on new biblical principles.

This revolutionary sexual ethic, which Noyes introduced in 1846, was the source of his converts and the tenet that gave Oneida its distinctive flavor among the numerous utopian experiments. "The new commandment is that we love one another, not by pairs, as in the world, but en masse." Sexual exclusiveness had been abolished and a method instituted whereby individuals were freed to have sexual intercourse with any partner who so desired. Noyes rejected the notion that this was "free love" and insisted that he advocated social, rather than sexual control. One important aspect of the complex marriage system was the concept of an "ascending and descending" fellowship that encouraged novices to have intercourse with those who were above them spiritually. Physically, the same principle was applied so that young men who had not mastered the principles of male continence would be initiated by women who had passed their menopause. As time passed, the ascending and descending fellowship brought together the youngest and oldest, because the leaders were acknowledged to be spiritually superior. It was agreed that "all should associate with those who draw them upward."

Noyes had worked out a plan whereby individuals could improve their spiritual state, and young members, in particular, were encouraged to associate with community members who had achieved a high degree of personal perfection. In turn, the older members were expected to guide and instruct new members along the path of perfection. An example of the impact of the ascending-descending relationship can be seen in the following excerpt from a young woman's journal taken from the Oneida period.

> From a deceitful weak woman , he has transformed me by his grace, into a sincere strong one (comparatively) and given me power to conquer many difficulties in my mind. He has given me companionship and fellowship with Mr.Noyes, that advances my education - enlarges my heart and mind, and enables me to converse with my superiors as I never dreamed before.

In theory, such a relationship moved individuals from a sinful state towards the perfection of the Primitive Church. "True circulation requires that love should take an upward direction, from the young toward the old, the immature toward the experienced, the less spirited toward the more spiritual." Community critics charged that the ascending-descending relationship was simply a device employed by the older members (mostly men) to obtain young companions. In its defense the colony argued that all sexual proposals had to go through a third party, and younger members were free to refuse any offer. What the ascending-descending relationship did accomplish was to keep both prestige and authority in the hands of the older members. The latter believed in a biblical tradition, resisted change, and eventually came in conflict with a generation that was scientifically minded and removed from a patriarchal biblical tradition.

The other sexual aspect of the complex marriage system that had a bearing on the social life of the community was the distinction Noyes made between what he termed the "amative" and the "propagative" functions of sexual intercourse. He believed the "amative," or social side of intercourse, superior to the "propagative" side because the expenditure of the seed in the propagative method could produce unwanted children, and Noyes was opposed to "excessive random procreation." Ordinary sexual intercourse, he wrote, "without the intention of procreation, is probably to be classed with masturbation." Noyes was closer in this respect to the Shaker position than to that of the reformer Robert Dale Owen, who favored the withdrawal method over either abstinence or Noyes's male continence. The self-control method of male continence, in which the male did not reach orgasm, but satisfied himself with the earlier stages of intercourse, heightened the amative functions of intercourse and did not carry with it the problem of childbearing. Noyes hoped that the principles of male continence and amative intercourse could one day have a place among the fine arts and that it would "rank above music, painting, sculpture for it combines the charms and benefits of them all." Members of the community were urged to place emphasis on the amative side of intercourse and view it as "a joyful act of fellowship." In placing their emphasis on the "fellowship" of sex, these "communists" attempted to place their own sexual life in service to a corporate mission.

In September 1852 Noyes delivered one of his home talks that has failed to appear in any of the various anthologies of his writings. The title was "Practical Suggestions for Regulating Intercourse of the Sexes." I quote it in its entirety because these were the rules Oneida members followed throughout much of their history.

1. The Sexes should sleep apart. Their coming together should not be to sleep but to edify and enjoy. Sleeping is essentially an individual function that precludes sociability. Probably the truest fashion would be not only for the sexes but for those of the same sex to sleep apart. We need not insist upon reform to this extent until convenient, but for the sake of love it is best that the sexes should ordinarily sleep apart. Overfamiliarity dulls the edges of sexual passion.

2. Proposals for love interviews are best made not directly but through a third party. This method is favorable to modesty and also to freedom. It allows of refusals without embarassment. If the third party is a superior, as it should be, one in whom the lovers have confidence, calm wisdom will enter, as it should, to give needed advice and prevent inexpediencies. The third party will also be helpful in arrangements. This method excludes selfish privacy and makes love a Community affair.

3. Short interviews will be found the best. Lovers should come together for an hour or two, and should separate to sleep. If they part before over-excitement, they will think of each other with pleasure afterwards. It is an excellent rule to leave the table while the appetite is still good.

4. It is not according to truthful taste to spend much time in talk. The tongue has its field to itself all day. Why not the other members have their turn ? I imagine that the impotence, which some men complain of, may be connected with over-activity of the tongue.

5. Cultivate the habit of sagacious, reflective observation. In the midst of passion watch for improvement. So shall the spirit of truth go with you and perfect you in the heavenly art.

The Perfectionists who worked out the plan were not evil men, hamstrung by ties of sin, but regenerate men, perfect in

their dedication to an Almighty plan. As such, these residents
of Putney, and later Oneida, were taught to believe that they
were part of God's plan to form a union on earth that other
men could observe and copy. Noyes himself was the key to
this new definition of sexual conduct, which he expressed as
early as 1840. "If God only can properly give a license to copu-
late, lewdness, fornication and adultery, may take place under cover of the ordinary license from man. Or, on the other
hand it is conceivable that persons may have a license from
God who have none from man : but in this case they will have
to prove their license. And thirdly, God's license and man's
may coincide, which is the most desireable." Noyes had
proved himself at Putney. The sense of dedication and the
messianic spirit of the residents are clearly revealed in some
correspondence between two community workers early in the
history at Oneida.

> Dear C——, I was thinking this morning of a love token
> you sent yesterday and it occurred to me that I might show
> my love for you by giving you a little advice. You are just
> beginning to be a lover and want to be a true one. Let me
> now advise you in the first place that love and work belong
> together and are to be thoroughly mixed in the union which
> God is forming among us. Just so far as you are a true lover
> you will be a faithful worker. Learn to despise any love that
> unmans you or makes you slack in business or improve-
> ment. Love is a science and God is calling you to study it,
> and is offering to help us, in theory and in practice. Let us
> walk worthy of our vocation.
> Yours for improvement."

Both the scientific and practical aspects of life and love in
community, as outlined by the letter, reflect the virtues that
the community's membership embodied. Of course there were
periods when that mission was clouded by disputes, dissension, and revolts; yet this messianic vision (both at Putney
and at Oneida) brought people together and kept them engaged. The inauguration of the radical sexual system of male
continence did not diminish the religious or social faith of the
Putney Perfectionists in Noyes; they rallied to his support

and "enthusiastically" (he reported) adopted the plan. Noyes took as his first mate in his new system Mary Cragin, and out of this union came a set of twins—presumably planned. The townspeople of Putney reacted with less enthusiasm; the grand jurors of Windham County charged that Noyes had committed adultery with two other members of the community, and on October 26, 1847, he was brought before Justice of the Peace Royall Tyler and charged with adultery.

This particular episode ended the sojourn at Putney, with Noyes fleeing the state rather than face the charges and a jail term. Leaving his followers to face the wrath of the people of Putney, he began to gather support in central New York to continue the work begun in Vermont. Although he was hounded out of Vermont as the result of his sexual philosophy rather than his religious zeal, Noyes had accomplished a great deal of practical community building during the period. He had laid the theological and philosophical foundations of the his community; had found a nucleus of believers and supporters who would follow him and his messianic message; had, through the periodicals, found an audience for his religious and social views.

The transition from Putney to Oneida was difficult on several grounds: there were members who resisted the complex marriage idea and Noyes's liaison with Mary Cragin, and those splits were resolved over time; but in 1850–1852 there were still members living in marriage according to the world's definition. Writing from Brooklyn in 1850, Noyes touched on another issue, the "unmarried men" problem. "The transition of the young men from the hot blood of virginity to the quiet freedom which is the essential element of our Society is emphatically the difficult pass in our social experience. . . . the plan proposed last fall of introducing the young men to the freedom of the Association through the more spiritual women has been attended with difficulties. Mrs. Cragin lost her equilibrium in the attempt to carry it out, and there appears to have been an unhealthy excitement in Perkins (James) and perhaps others, which has ended in grudging and discontent" (March 4, 1850). But Noyes persevered. For some the whole experience of complex marriage was a calming one. One member wrote to his brother in 1852 about how his "amativeness" had been curbed. "I was to some extent addicted to the practice of masturbation. I can say with a thankful heart, that the influences of free love have cured me of that evil and made me entirely free from inordinate excitement" (Joseph Skinner to Alan Skinner, March 30, 1852).

Noyes's education at Dartmouth, Andover, and Yale, his religious conversion, his periods of remorse and temptation, his publishing ventures, his preaching, his proselytizing, and his Perfectionism—all these were part of his theological and social development from Andover to Putney, a prelude to Oneida. At the time of the dispersal from Putney the community consisted of twenty-one adults and ten children. Most of the adults were between the ages of twenty-five and thirty-five. The community's material assets consisted of two houses, a store, a printing office, and some twelve thousand dollars in the bank. Over half the residents were from Putney and the rest from Perfectionist strongholds in northern Vermont and from around Belchertown, Massachusetts. It was never a community in any formal sense, rather a collection of Perfectionists who, in the interest of religious and social expediency, had come together in southern Vermont. The community at Oneida, however, would not be a loose congregation but a cohesive and successful combination of "Bible Communism" and a form of utopianism that drew on a number of radical reforms of the period.

The growth and development of the Oneida Community from 1848 to 1880 was governed by a variety of forces, not the least of which was Noyes's capacity to mold effectively the forces that led his followers to Madison County, New York. For the bulk of the individuals who came during the first five years not only remained, but represented the dominant leadership until the 1870s. Since the Putney community had been effectively dissolved by the adultery charges of October 1847, Noyes needed a new home for his utopian mission. After visiting a farm owned by a Perfectionist believer near Syracuse, Noyes became convinced that the adjoining land should be the home of the Putney Perfectionists.

In March 1848 the Noyes and Cragin families joined other

local believers at the farm, and the Oneida Community began its first year. The section to which the settlers had come lay at the geographic center of New York State. On the twenty-three acres Noyes purchased there was a hut built by some Indians, a small shoemaker's shop, and a wood lot. The state, which had purchased the rich farmland a few years earlier, required only that the settlers maintain the tax assessment. The wood lot and Jacob Burt's sawmill provided the means by which Oneida began construction of the New Jerusalem. By May 1848 the group numbered fifty-one, all dedicated to the divine mission of Noyes and the promise of the Oneida Community. The men who joined the society were not poets or political anarchists; they were farmers and mechanics who knew how to run a mill, plow a field, and lay a foundation.

The settlers were, in the main, a young group, with more than 80 percent of them below the age of forty; Noyes was then thirty-seven. Approximately 85 percent came from Vermont, New York, and Massachusetts, with New York providing a little under half that total. Congregationalists predominated, followed by Methodists, Presbyterians, Dutch Reformed, Baptists, and Quakers. A variety of trades were represented, giving the community an artisan base necessary for the forging of a society in the wilderness. There were farmers (a majority), carpenters, machinists, millers, and school teachers. There can be no doubt that the great revivals of the thirties and forties were the initial impulse that started the members on the road to Oneida. Noyes's own religious conversion had come in 1831 as part of the influential Charles Finney revival, and his religious pilgrimage from that point on was similar to that of many of his disciples. The "new measure" techniques of protracted meetings, excited sermons, and physical exercises created a frenzied atmosphere that disrupted church organization and led to new liturgical forms.

William H. Perry was one of the early settlers and described his own religious development. "Born in the County of Oneida near Utica Feb. 13, 1806. Converted and united with the Congregational Church in Chittenango in 1832. After passing through a series of revival sessions in the New Measure School and on hearing of the New Haven Perfectionists professing to live holy lives free from sin, my mind became very much excercised on the subject." Few of the first members had been untouched by the revivals, and some had embraced the doctrines of one of the radical groups. The case of Riley Burnham is exemplary.

> Joined the Congregational church at Middlebury, Vermont at the age of 17. After become disaffected toward the church and passing through the baptism of Millerism, he set himself in earnest to seek the truth. Commenced reading the Putney testimony, and about a year and a half since he became willing to be called Perfectionist and made a confession of Christ. In coming here his feelings were that he wanted to be be where he could have his faults told him in faithfulness. His confidence in the association has been increasing since he came.

Another product of the Millerite and Adventist agitation in 1843–1844 concerning the "last days" excitement was Sophrina Clarke, who indicated a need to acquiesce to something more enduring than a momentary religious ecstasy: "Born in Wallingford, Connecticut. Married at the age of 19. Joined the Baptist Church in Wallingford, Connecticut at the age of 17. Was inclined to Millerism as its first appearance, and passed from that into Perfectionism through the influence of her sister and the Perfectionist writings three or four years since. She maintained her confidence through the storms of the Putney dispersion, and has looked forward to union with the association with great desire. She loves to learn and expects to give up her own will."

The connection between the Millerite upheaval and the origins of the Oneida Community should not be exaggerated—rather considered in the perspective of contemporary interest in revivalism, Fourierism, the communitarian social philosophy of the eccentric Frenchman, Charles Fourier, and millenarianism. Whether by "conversation," "preaching," "testimony," or "personal instruction," the early members had moved away from orthodoxy into radical groups, often Perfectionist. It was no easy task to go back to a settled church after a conversion experience: "Like climbers advancing on a mountain ridge, they either attained a new reach of broader ground, retreat or fall into the abyss below," Whitney Cross noted in *The Burned-Over District* (Ithaca, 1950). Furthermore, he wrote that the "Oneida Community saved some from that abyss by offering theological and social security." The case of Alma Burnham was typical. "Born in Cambridge, Vermont. Joined the Congregational Church at the age of twenty-five. Embraced Perfectionism in 1844. While in a state of hungering and thirsting after righteousness, she cast her eye on something in the Perfectionist paper, which had been before disposed to avoid as error. This met her feelings and attracted her to the truth. The name 'Perfectionist' bore a great reproach in Cambridge, and it was hard for her to forsake the ordinance of a respectable religion, but she gradually became willing to give up everything, and made an open confession of Christ. She felt quiet and at home in the association and had confidence they would do right and correct her imperfections in love and justice."

Obviously, there were those who joined for specific sexual reasons, but they seem in a distinct minority. Noyes's reputation as a faith healer attracted a few members, but the dominant note within these early spiritual autobiograhies is one of a search for security amidst pain and illness. Why, then, did members turn to Oneida and not to another communal group? At least two reasons emerge clearly to explain the source of the move to Oneida rather than to some other sect. First, members had been touched at some point by Noyes's preaching, or more important, they had read and reflected on Noyes's writings—usually, in his periodicals.

The domestic life out of which Oneida's membership came was one not of stability, but of frantic religious and social upheaval. For some, the periodical sustained them in their religious isolation over a long period and through difficult moments. George Campbell's journey from orthodox religion to the community at Oneida is an example of the periodical's influence.

Born in Orange, N.J. Became a member of the Presbyterian Church in Newark, N.J. in August, 1837. About two years after he was converted to Oberlinism, a moderate form of Perfectionism, and went to the revivalistic Free Church in the latter place. Shortly thereafter, in 1839–40, received some of the writings of J.H.Noyes and became a believer in his testimony, and has been a constant reader of the Putney publications ever since. Made a full confession of Christ in August, 1848.

In the case of Campbell there is no indication of Millerite frenzy, or of a desire for personal security, rather, there is a slow movement toward a new commitment based on personal holiness. His odyssey was carried on within the revival tradition; it was the newspaper that moved him beyond that experience and into Oneida. The bond that *The Perfectionist* created among the first settlers was considerable, and Noyes realized the importance of the paper. It was more than a religious sheet; it was a continuing focus of activity throughout the community's history. Noyes devoted the bulk of his time to the paper and believed it the greatest single contribution to the association's life. Without it Noyes would have been just another revivalist working the Burned-Over District.

During the early 1850s Noyes had great faith in the power of the press to bring about a social and religious revolution. He had seen the effects of Brisbane's column in Greeley's *New York Tribune* and was pleased to see Brook Farm "converted" to Fourierism in 1844. If Brisbane could bring about the socialist revolution through a newspaper column then why could not John H. Noyes initiate the same revolution for "Bible Communism" from Madison County? He was a confirmed religious publicist and propagandist.

A second major factor in attracting (and maintaining) members to the Oneida association was Noyes's ability to convey a convincing and reassuring social scheme. The first members did not believe they had joined an "experimental" community, but rather one in which the heavenly model had been conceived, then put forward; only willing hands were needed to put it to work. "So the true plan of Association, about which many in these days are busily scheming, is not a matter of future discovery and experiment. The church of the first born has been for ages working out in theory and practice, all the problems of social science. If Fourier has had access to the heavenly model, and based his motives on the actual experiments of the citizens of the New Jerusalem, his system will stand. If not, it will be consumed when the fire shall try everyman's work."

As a knowledgeable observer of American socialism, Noyes knew that many utopian experiments had failed because they followed solely an agriculturally based economy that could not support them. It was his belief that for a communal group to be successful it "ought to keep near the centres of business." His analysis of Owenism and Fourierism emphasized that both movements were based on "the enlargement of the home—the extension of family union beyond the little man-wife circle to large corporations." By this statement he meant that it was necessary to return to a home-based economy that was, in many ways, preindustrial, while at the same time taking advantage of certain large-scale efficiencies offered by corporate living. This communal "home" would humanize the industrial process by combining elements of work, play, and family life under one roof. Noyes proposed to substitute what he called the "family relation" for a system of hiring; business was to be sanctified by making it an extension of the home and by spiritualizing "degrading" labor in this new family.

Oneida offered the "unitary family," which combined the social, economic, religious, and educational functions of society under the family banner. The "one home and one family relation" refrain found in the community hymn was not only a spiritual one, but an economic one. Members worked and produced products for the market because of Christian communism, not capitalist individualism. "With unity of heart and interest, and free hands instead of indifferent hirelings, anything can be done in the line of hospitality, that is reasonable to undertake, and done with the greatest universal pleasure."

Labor could be made attractive if it were part of a larger commitment that included the "four great interests of mankind—business, family affection, education and religion" joined together "wherever human beings have a home." Such a community, whether large or small, could become a school in which the members learned to elevate their spiritual, social, and economic condition within the framework of community devotion. In this "community school" there would be "a free and cordial mingling of the sexes, in nearly all kinds of employment . . . no hirelings or masters, and no money or thoughts of money between the workman." Thus, the motive of industry would not be "the sordid one of necessity, but primarily the real attraction of art." Sordid sex and sordid money had been banished from this Eden.

Whenever the community received a large order for one of its products, or when harvesting season approached, the whole community participated in a "bee." Work was expected to take on a gamelike atmosphere, as the young and the old, the ascending and the descending, the leaders and the followers were released from their ordinary jobs to tackle a single task. As a result the work was accomplished in a shorter period of time, workers engaged in varied forms of labor, and the common cause of the kingdom of God was furthered. This corporate involvement—represented by the work bee—permeated the total life of the society.

The association remained flexible for both social and economic reasons, with the economic rationale for such flexibility intended to buttress their precarious enterprise. During the first seven years Oneida bordered on bankruptcy a number of times, with labor shifted, then consolidated in order to respond to temporary economic demands. The membership was instructed to keep "open to new influences," and to avoid stifling regimentation. "We are out upon routine and bores, and are set upon learning to shift our sails for the breeze of inspiration." Because of the vicissitudes of the market the "Communists" were often required to adjust to the wind or be swamped. Jobs were rotated "so that all have a variety of occupations, and an opportunity to find out what each one is best adapted to."

This rotation of labor reaffirmed the belief that each individual was part of a larger scheme. At the same time, members did not become overly attached to their particular jobs and were not permitted to cultivate a "selfish" attitude. During a beeing session individuals had to put aside their particular tasks and devote their energies to a project that served a larger interest—the economic health of the association. Such corporate activity forced members to work in a manner that Noyes claimed was based on a "gregarious, chivalric principle." Here is but one example of the cohesive quality generated by a "bee": "Ten acres of corn have thus been stacked by volunteers of the Community in half a day, and sport made of it. To draw this corn from the field . . . would be a long and tedious job for one or two; but the Association can accomplish it at the right time . . . with much more enthusiasm and sportive feeling of a game of ball." Such sport not only provided diversification of labor, but equipped the association with a body of workers who could fill any job when necessary. One has only to look at the various jobs held by members over a twenty-year period to realize the partial success of the society in job diversification. In one case an individual was listed as a blacksmith in 1850, a machinist in 1870, and a dentist in 1880—were they not allied but diverse trades? In practice there were still jobs in which women predominated, such as domestic affairs, and those that men continued to ply—business affairs.

A new member in 1853 put the ideological point clearly. The family (which encompassed the economic, social, and intellectual life of the community) had been merged with the religious or revival spirits: "Here the *family* and *church* [italics in original] are united. They congregate every evening in the week, not for formal, legal worship, but for social benefit; and to speak as the 'Spirit of Truth' giveth utterance. They also devote a certain portion of each day to intellectual cultivation. Think of always living in such a school." An account, published in 1855, of how an "average" day was spent at the colony and the reaction of one individual to his or her duties and responsibilities, offers an excellent example of both communal dedication and labor diversity. After having a simple breakfast, the colonist engaged in a "Bible game, then read proofs for the *The Circular*. The tedious task of proofreading went on for only an hour, and then the colonist was

free to spend some time as he or she wished—in this case
writing some letters. After dinner there was more reading,
followed by a communal "carpet bag bee" that was both social
and practical; then a trip to the woodlot. Finally, and here we
have the most revealing comment on the day's activity, the
worker engaged in self-castigation and recrimination because
he or she had "loitered unprofitably" and "took a nap." It
seems doubtful that there were more than a few such moments for anyone in the association, since loitering was kept
to a minimum; a Puritan conscience was always a stern
guide.

After supper there was still time for a committee session,
a self-improvement class in Greek, and again, some communal involvement in the evening meeting. To end the evening,
and possibly to atone for the "unprofitable loitering," this dedicated worker volunteered to help prepare breakfast. The
worker was probably a woman. Yet we see this dedication to
satisfying group work everywhere. For example, resolutions
were passed urging that "women should not let a day pass
without engaging in manly," that is, physical work, since
"love and work belong together and are to be thoroughly
mixed in the union God is forming among us."

This combination of religious dedication and socialist
"spontaneity" created an atmosphere of intense relaxation.
Members were expected to read or to play chess or a musical
instrument in order to show their desire for "self-improvement." Such activities were always tempered by the goals and
demands of community life. For example, a young musician
was criticized in October 1856 because he had let his music
interfere with the harmony of the group. "He was thought to
be energetic and persevering with a purpose to improve, and
make the most of himself; but not sufficiently docile, tractable
and prompt to yield to the desires of others."

The "desires of others" were important in this communal
society, particularly when the association had set goals that
transcended the immediate needs of one individual. There
was a real loss of self for individuals when they merged their
poetic and practical inspiration into something greater, something called rather sentimentally, "one home and one family

relation." Music, art, literature, and the theater were encouraged because they elevated the spiritual senses; whereas to-
bacco, pork, extravagant dress, and personal luxury were
discouraged because they catered to the base and the sensual
instincts of man. The Grahamite influence can be seen most
directly here.

Oneida's prosperity came as the result of both the mundane manufacturing of traps and traveling bags and the ability to temper its altruistic ideals to a world of profit and loss.
By elevating and spiritualizing their work, the members were
able to create a society that was agreeable *and* profitable.
Their business success went beyond the mere accumulation of
money in order to clothe and to feed themselves; their success
represented a triumph, for Christ, over the forces of Mammon,
whose emissaries had corrupted and defeated the world, but
not Oneida. In September 1854 *The Circular* summed up the
relationship between the community's utopian goals and its
business ethic.

> The expansion of business, in the right spirit, is to us a to-
> ken of God's advancing conquest of the world. In the com-
> munity business is kept pure and made acceptable to
> God. . . . So far as business proceeds from a new center—the
> power driving the machinery is different from that of the
> world; as our points of contact increase, we shall expect to
> see one kind of business "cog in" until the whole business
> world is won over to Christ.

Another key to success lay in industrial flexibility, since
the community engaged in a variety of commercial enter-
prises that indicated its resourcefulness and the keen spirit of
the members. Like the Shakers, they had engaged in commercial trade in order to bring sorely needed cash into the society.
They made extensive use of mechanical devices to ease the
burdens of labor but refused (at least for part of their history)
to have any of their inventions patented. A patent assumed
"exclusive" control over a product, and such an act was incon-
sistent with the communist's ideal of free and equal access to
the fruits of labor.

Begun in 1855, the trap business was a model of segmented cooperative effort. Men forged the steel parts, women put the chain links together on each trap, and young boys (when not in school) did piecemeal work. Pierrepont Noyes's own account of his occasional duties in the chain shop during the 1870s points up this corporate involvement. "The Community evidently believed that children should work. Every day except Sunday, we make chains for an hour after lunch . . . . We children thought we were making all the chains used and considered ourselves important factors in the business." The success of the trap-making operation forced the community to repudiate its theory of free labor because demand for the traps became so great that Oneida was forced to hire workers from the surrounding area, beginning in 1863. At one point, the community was unable to fill orders for some ninety thousand traps (many of them rat traps), and by 1865 the bulk of labor, in both the trap and the bag business, was done by the "hirelings" while the Perfectionists supervised them.

Noyes feared the contaminations of the American business system; he made his salesmen undergo a "defumigation," as he called it, both spiritual and physical, when they returned from a business trip. (In the 1870s, the construction of a Turkish bath aided in the physical part of the rehabilitation, and throughout the community's history the process of "mutual criticism," or group faultfinding, completed the process.)

With its economic base secured through the production of traps the colony was then able to build some impressive new dwellings, to continue its periodicals (they always lost money), and to begin educating its members at prestigious colleges and universities. Although Noyes had been forced to flee Vermont and sought refuge in central New York, Oneida was a society that was in vital contact with the world around it. The Midland Railroad passed nearby, bringing with it both visitors and potential members. Between 1864 and 1875 at least a dozen young men attended university, with Yale's Sheffield School a favorite, and some even toured the Continent during summers. Theodore Noyes—John Humphrey's son—attended Yale Medical School and returned to the colony a Comtean and a eugenics proponent. In 1868 the membership at Oneida stood at 210, with 44 in Wallingford, Connecticut, and 16 at the mercantile office in New York City. It was in that year that the Democratic party offered the community $800,000 to turn the buildings at Oneida into a soldiers' home; a confident colony rejected the offer. Within the association, activities continued in much the fashion as in previous years. Outside the colony, events could not have been more auspicious because Noyes's cousin, Rutherford B. Hayes, occupied the governor's chair in Ohio and said publicly that he "had no prejudices on account of the colony's religious beliefs." That was in 1868.

In 1869 John H. Noyes ushered in a new era in the march toward the heavenly kingdom with a remarkable but predictable use of a journalistic metaphor: "Education is waiting for its printing press, and its printing press is to be scientific propagation." The kingdom that Noyes had envisaged in 1848 had been slow in coming, with the world seemingly heedless of the Perfectionist message that poured forth from the presses at Oneida and from a branch at Wallingford, Connecticut. The twenty-three year period at Oneida had not been an unqualified success, since the money lost on a colony in Brooklyn in the early 1850s and on a business agency in Manhattan in the 1860s had slowed their progress. In addition, the influence of the all-important periodicals was often imperceptible, and their publication was always a costly operation.

Although Noyes believed that the time was propitious for the institution of a variant on his advanced sexual scheme, time was also running out; he was now fifty-eight. A shortcut had to be found that would ensure the success of the experiment begun in 1848. Noyes and the other leaders wished to see some additional, tangible proof that their hopes for the production of the "new man" had not been in vain. For the stirpiculture experiment would not only provide additional members to swell the ranks, but would go a long way towards perfecting the world both spiritually and physically.

Noyes maintained that the stirpiculture plan naturally grew from the complex marriage system, but there is no doubt that his decision to inaugurate the change came at the urging of a dozen or so young men who, during the late sixties and early seventies, returned from medical college and scientific studies at Yale and elsewhere. The writings of Thomas Huxley and the logic of the Darwinian argument impressed this younger generation. Noyes himself was not hostile to their new ideas. "Let us of the Oneida Community consider it our business to pioneer in this direction and get ready for the world, when it shall come to this inevitable crisis [exploding population]. The question in any case may not be solely what sort of offspring will be the result, but what will be the effect on the social relation of the parties . . . . In other words social considerations may be complicated with personal ones thus making the problem of selection far more intricate for human beings than for horses."

Noyes's realization that the selection process for humans would be "more intricate" than one for animals did not sway him from his course of action. As he stated in his *Essay on Scientific Propagation,* "duty is plain; we say we ought to do it - we must do it ; but we cannot. The law of God urges us on; but society holds us back. . . . The boldest course is the safest." The bold course was taken, although the problems which would arise from the experiment were not obvious in 1869.

Hilda Herrick Noyes and George Wallingford Noyes, writing in 1923, outlined the reasons why the experiment was begun. First, the complex marriage arrangement permitted flexibility in mating. Second, the community had both sufficient income and members to undertake the experiment. Third, there were capable leaders, and the membership had confidence in those leaders. Fourth, the sexual system of male continence permitted the continuance of normal sex life, even if the individual did not take part in the stirpiculture plan. Fifth, and most important, there was still extraordinary religious devotion. "These characteristics made a large majority of the community members fervently desireous not only to avoid selfishness, but positively to engage with all their powers in any enterprise which they thought in the interest of the Kingdom of God."

Participants in the experiment were chosen for their "spiritual, intellectual and moral" qualities. From 1869 to 1875 the direction of the experiment was in the hands of the so-called central members of the Community. In January, 1875 a formal Stirpiculture Committee of six men and six women was set up in order to determine fitness and to select participants. This group functioned for about fifteen months, that is, until April 1876, when the selection process was returned to the central committee.

Noyes's call to those who "loved science well enough" to make themselves "eunuches for the Kingdom of Heaven's sake" was answered by at least fifty-three young women and thirty-eight men, and they took part in the initial experiment. The following resolution, signed by the original group of women before entering into "the scientific union," combines scientific and religious logic.

> 1. That we do not belong to ourselves in any respect, but that we belong to God, and second to Mr. Noyes as God's true representative;
> 2. That we have no rights or personal feelings in regard to child bearing which shall in the least degree oppose or embarrass [sic] him in his choice of scientific combinations;
> 3. That we will put aside all envy, childishness and self seeking and rejoice in those who are chosen candidates; and that we will, if necessary, become martyrs to science, and cheerfully resign all desire to become mothers, if for any reason Mr.Noyes deem us unfit material for propagation. Above all, we offer ourselves "living sacrifices" to God and true communism.

Nowhere is the sense of commitment to the society and its goals more explicitly revealed than in that statement. Noyes was able, in numerous situations, to dictate the destiny of community members, as we have seen, through a system of mutual criticism, ascending and descending spiritual and sexual relationships, and finally, through his role as chosen prophet of God. In retrospect, there is a certain coldness about the young women's statement that they "have no right to personal feelings," but when placed within the framework of a millennial faith in Oneida and the New Jerusalem, their dedication becomes understandable.

Application to participate in the experiment was made to

the committee by couples who desired to become parents, and in due time the committee either accepted or rejected them. If the application was vetoed, then the board attempted to find another suitable combination agreeable to all parties. According to the study made by Hilda Herrick Noyes and George W. Noyes in 1929, during a typical fifteen-month period, fifty-one applications were received, of which all but nine were accepted. It is important to note, however, that approximately 25 percent of the matches were brought about at the initiative of the committee.

During the first six years the elder Noyes personally chose the participants in the experiment on the basis of their leadership qualities and religious experience. The fact that the men in the experiment were, on average, twelve years older than the women indicated that the male community leaders played a prominent role in the experiment. It is also interesting to note that, of the fifty-eight children born under the plan, twenty-eight, or 48 percent, were fathered by ten men. There is no indication in the available records as to who the ten men were, except that it is known that Noyes fathered nine of the stirpiculture children. But on the basis of information about those who did participate and the fact that spiritual rather than physical criteria were used indicates the old rather than the young were the progenitors of the new race. That distinctions were made between the spiritual and the scientific is demonstrated by Theodore Noyes's suggesting the names (in 1876) of eight men who—"from a scientific standpoint"—could be the father of Tirzah Miller's third child. The top three were: G. D. Allen (thirty-eight); J. B. Herrick (thirty-nine); Homer Barron (forty-one). She was then thirty-three. She did have a child by J. B. Herrick, whom she married, and subsequently had another child with him after the breakup.

The central question for me is not who fathered the majority of the children, but rather why did the community eventually revolt against the scheme? Initially, they had placed a great deal of faith in Noyes's ability to lead and direct the community operation, but by 1874 certain groups had begun to question the wisdom of his leadership. The key to this disaffection on the part of some of the members lies in the dual nature of Oneida's success as a utopian venture. Its success lay in its ability to communicate to its members a corporate sense of involvement on both the social and the utopian levels. The social area included the day-to-day involvement of the members in the affairs of the society. The utopian element embraced a sense of mission that suggested Oneida's peculiar spiritual contribution to the world, really independent of any organization, namely, "Bible Communism." From 1848 to 1868 each member of the association had been involved on both levels, thus, at least temporarily, having the best of both worlds at Oneida. Beginning in 1869, however, with the stirpiculture experiment, the corporate effort was replaced by an exclusive one in several ways. First, the effort placed the scientifically oriented generation in a prominent position, for their pet theories had been adopted. Second, it placed the community elders in an "exclusive" position since they were naturally to be the fathers of the new race. Third, it denied equal participation in the experiment, thus alienating some elements within the younger generation and those who did not measure up to the "spiritual" standard set by Noyes's informal central committee. Fourth, once begun it raised the specter that there were those within Oneida who wished to "regularize" their preferred sexual arrangements. In short, couples wanted to get married.

Aside from the divisive character of the plan, there was another component linked to the stirpiculture plan—the problem of transferral of authority within the society. It seems obvious that the genius of Noyes lay in the category of what has been called "charismatic" leadership. He exerted his leadership in such a way that he was both part of the community and separate from it. The association at Oneida followed his guidance, not because he had, in the language of Max Weber, "traditional" or "legal authority," but because he was viewed as a link in a spiritual chain that began with Jesus Christ and St. Paul. Noyes's relationship with the group was an ambiguous one in that he often removed himself from the community and lived apart from it; however, that aloofness was an element in the power of his charismatic leadership. Theodore Noyes's role in the disintegration of the colony was a major one. As Constance Noyes Robertson has shown, he was a confused, contradictory, and autocratic man who had lost his faith in his father's "Bible Communism" and tried to substitute for it Comteanism and Spiritualism, neither powerful enough to guide the colony through difficult times. Caught in this clash of history, personalities, and shifting ideology were the common followers at Oneida. One such individual, Victor Hawley, has left us an extraordinary account of how those shifting forces bore down on him. It is a love story that focuses on one fact: his desire to have a child with Mary Jones. This diary covers two years in the life of a man caught in the middle of an experiment in American community that tested its participants in a way that few communities have. It was at Oneida where the demands of a self competed with the demands of a society in the most intimate and deep fashion; it was a place where public life demanded the diminution of private interests; and it was a place where love and the demands of the flesh were tested.

CHAPTER TWO

Love Thy Scepter, Trust Thy Rod

I believe that the moral habits of heaven will come down upon us through the women.

—John H. Noyes,
"Women the More Civilized" (1864)

"Whom do I tell when I tell a blank page," Virginia Woolf wrote when she came to reflect on the art of diary keeping. That art has had a long and distinguished history, and its practitioners range from Samuel Pepys to anonymous schoolgirls. The habit of diary keeping was encouraged by seventeenth-century Puritans to intensify self-scrutiny in the pursuit of a perfected life; it was used by explorers and entrepreneurs to record travels and misadventures. It has included a rendering of the facts of public life and private diplomatic intrigue by the powerful; it has been a cry of conscience from the hearts of men and women searching for social redress; it has been a personal memorandum intended to detail the facts of common experience and daily life by simple people. Diaries, according to Thomas Mallon, whose *A Book of One's Own* is our most sensitive study of diaries, are "queer, ad hoc, private" efforts at what Aram Saroyan called, in response to his father's diary, "willed immortality."

Beyond that assessment, diaries have been called a "scrapbook of the self," and one critic has said that the "imprint a person leaves in a diary, like a fingerprint on a page, is a unique and intimate miniature." Generally, they seem fragile to the touch and are unlike many other historical records because of their distinct, personal and self-reflective character. Amiel, the great French diarist, described his own record in telling words. For him it was "my companion, my society, my confidant, my consolation, my memory, the hearer of my burdens, my echo, the reservoir of my inner experiences, my psychological itinerary." Sometimes called a resource for the lonely or a good companion, the diary is available when no other ear is present. Writing about English diarists, Robert Fothergill has noted that the constant process of "rendering version of oneself" to a blank page relieves the writer of some of the pain felt by an unexpressed self.

Certain kinds of diaries (what Fothergill calls "the soliloquy diary") reveal a constant rendering of self in both actual and imagined form. There is a continuous battle between a self, or a life, that seeks an outlet for expression and the daily account of that struggle. Questions like: "What am I becoming?" or "What will I make of myself?" are often written as a dramatic monologue, and they often constitute the core of such diaries. In such narratives there is a constant dialogue between certain external facts—"slept only an hour"—and the feelings that have been generated by internal longings: "Shall I never take a ride with thee again, Mary?" As such the diary forms the basis for the emergence of a new "self" in the world.

As a rule diaries deal with the particular, the mundane; Victor Hawley's follows that pattern but with one major exception—his life was lived within an extraordinary community. There are periods in his two-year account when little worth recording occurred, and yet, these commonplace events are dutifully reported. Then there are those days when the most intimate of thoughts, actions, and desires are jotted down. Few diaries have a self-conscious literary quality about them (Anaïs Nin's being the exception); yet stylistically, each has its own voice, and that voice becomes more apparent with every turn of the page.

"Clipped" is the best way to describe Victor Hawley's diary style. Obviously, he was uncomfortable with the page and unsure of his purpose in maintaining a diary, but his discomfort did not prevent him from interlacing the diary with soliloquies that reveal the depth of his feeling and his need to have someone become the "hearer of his burden." Despite his lack of literary ability, there are powerful sections—laments—that cry out for sympathy. When Hawley writes about a lost love, he writes like a man without a confidant; fortunately, he had his diary.

Peter Gay, in *The Bourgeois Experience: Education of the Senses* (New York, 1984), speaks of the diary as being a "resource of the lonely" and notes that in many cases these private journals are abandoned on marriage. And so it was with Victor Hawley; yet, during the two years he maintained it the diary served to sustain his fragile mind. The diary's importance lay in what it reveals not only about his private anxieties, but about the interrelatedness of his personal problems to issues that were central to Oneida: sexuality, love, community life, religious commitment. It is a case history that tells us a great deal about life at Oneida—particularly its emotional life—at a point when it was undergoing profound changes in its purpose and direction. Hawley's diary is filled with his innermost fears about his purpose, life, and future, and it reflects Oneida's own dilemmas. Hawley's own needs and those of the society clashed at a point when the boundaries of permissible activity were undergoing constant transformation. The diary reveals a conflict between a prideful sexuality that wanted love, children, and family and a scientific definition of sexuality that demanded restraint and self-denial. Oneida had been formed to combat the tendencies of the flesh, to channel sexuality so that it served rather than dominated. Cooperation, not competition—particulary in the sexual arena—was an essential ingredient of the new commonwealth.

Jesse Catherine Kinsley (who was nineteen at the time and had had her first sexual experience when she was sixteen) later wrote that the community leaders had tried to "forestall stolen loves" and "to make desire legitimate." It was the "purpose of those in authority—those who managed our lives—while in our hearts was innocence and struggle for unselfishness, and toward Mr.Noyes, loyalty as to one almost divine." Her own first love was romantic, but "at length I saw him become interested in a women greatly my superior in looks and in mentality, and because I would not then strive for what I thought would be selfishly sought, we drifted apart." Later, after the community breakup, she married Myron Kinsley, a leader much older than herself, and found "unreserved love." Before that marriage all of her loves had been "with reserve." "Surely," she wrote in a memoir to her daughter, "I was a Puritan *trained* [italics in original] to seek first the Kingdom of Heaven in every action." Her training had all been directed at denying self, at shaping her desires to conform to the wishes of those above her, her superiors.

At Oneida marriage had been, in John H. Noyes's words, "nailed to the cross"; with the inauguration of complex marriage at Putney and its denial of conventional practice, marriage had been replaced by a higher law. That law was the law of "Bible Communism," and it ruled Oneida for two decades. Nailing marriage to the cross was one thing and keeping it there another, particularly after the stirpiculture experiment had let loose the possibility of full coital enjoyment and children. By the 1870s the colony was a mature one and believed it had the intelligence and the will to keep procreation, licentiousness, and "exclusiveness" in check. Noyes had associated three evils with the world: "Excessive procreation, unbridled licentiousness and corrupting family life." Held in check for twenty years, these forces all broke forth with the introduction of the stirpiculture plan. When we look at Victor Hawley's diary, we can see how he was drawn toward those three evils.

The kind of perfection that Hawley sought represented just what the community had sought to repress. He desired the company of one woman, not a "community of interests"; he wanted a "special love." The diary began without preface or apologia in January 1876, and ended on December 19, 1877, without denouement. Hawley was faithful to his task of recording both the minutiae and the grand events of that period in his life, and significant gaps do not appear in the diary. It is composed of four natural sections, each punctuated by an important turning point in the Hawley-Jones romance. Victor Hawley's diary is primarily a record of his emotional state: his bouts with melancholia, his hypochondria, his anxiety. Beyond that chronicle there are comments about his work, his occasional excursions from Oneida, and his hobbies. Most of his notations, however, center on life within the society and on the traumas he experienced while in pursuit of his true and perfect love. Throughout the whole diary the figure of Mary Jones looms large, but fortunately, she did leave a few letters that describe her own moods and feelings.

The first part covers the period from January 1, 1876, to April 11, 1876, and in this section we are introduced to the cast of characters and the broad outlines of the problems Hawley would face during the next two years. Within this section there are also the greatest number of shorthand notations. His desire to keep his secret life truly secret resulted in his using shorthand, particularly when he wrote about sexual matters. His keeping parts of the diary in Munson would not have prevented anyone from deciphering it since the form was widely used within the community. He used the shorthand as a psychological device to describe what he could not admit to anyone else; to write about what could not be said. Later in the diary he virtually abandons its use; however, during the first months shorthand represented, in symbolic fashion, the core of his deviance from colony belief and practice.

Visitors to Oneida during this period were always impressed by the spacious lawns, by the ample accommodations, and by other manifestations of the colonists' achievements. These buildings represented the success of the colonists in the world and their material progress toward the New Jerusalem. They had begun their colony with modest structures, consisting of two simple farmhouses and some outbuildings. Over time they had constructed two "Mansion Houses" and a variety of industrial buildings to serve their growing needs. There was no single site plan that laid out their principles of design, rather, as Dolores Hayden writes in *Seven American Utopias* (Cambridge, 1976), it was a "synthesis of phalanstery plans by Charles Fourier . . . and designs by Robert Owen for villages of unity and mutual cooperation. Their physical environment had been adapted to their needs and was, at the same time, expressive of their peculiar philosophy." From the Fourierists they learned "about using circulation space to bring people together," and from the Shakers, utilized space to keep people separate.

The first Mansion House had been begun in 1848, and there were additions made to it in 1849, 1850, and 1851; and the second Mansion House was completed in 1862. In 1863 they constructed the "Tontine," which served as an all-purpose structure housing the kitchen, dining room, carpenter shop, trap shop, printing office, bag shop, fruit-preserving area, laundry, and, for a time, the silk industry. As the community grew, or as it altered its social plans, it made additions to its buildings. For example, an addition was built in 1869–1870 to the second Mansion House to accommodate the stirpiculture babies, and in 1877–1878 a new bedroom wing was added to house the young adults coming of age. An interior courtyard (the "Quadrangle") served as the focal point of this developing plan. The exteriors were all done in red brick with white wooden trim, and the roofs were slate. To the visitor it was an imposing though rambling collection of structures, but for the colonists it represented "successive stages of progress" in their efforts to create a new society.

Built in stages from 1861 to 1878, the second Mansion House served a variety of community purposes. On the first floor there were offices, library, sitting rooms, single and double bedrooms, a dining room (in the Tontine), a nursery, a children's parlor; the second floor was primarily bedrooms but also contained the meeting hall, stage, and upper sitting room; the third floor held additional bedrooms, the south tower, and the balcony of the meeting hall. Private bedrooms were, by the 1870s, available for most members, but they were not to be used as gathering places for groups—that was the function of the sitting rooms located near the bedroom areas. "The presence of communal activities outside bedroom door," Dolores Hayden notes, "obviated the possibility of loneliness for residents and at the same time decreased the possibility of exclusive arrangements." Bedroom doors could be observed from the sitting rooms with the result that "familial or sexual attachments could be easily discovered and discouraged."

The Upper Sitting Room was a place where members gathered for smaller meetings, such as entertainment put on by the children, whereas the Meeting Hall was the hub of their social life where general meetings, criticism sessions, and musical events occurred and where the people of Oneida congregated every evening. At first glance the arrangement of rooms, meeting halls, lounges, and bedrooms seems haphazard; however, the people exhibited a high degree of consciousness, according to Dolores Hayden, in designing these spaces.

> To describe and define the spaces within the Mansion so carefully and precisely, the Perfectionists needed to be extremely aware of the nuances of psychological responses evoked by the stimuli as the size of the tables, personal distances in meeting rooms, the warmth of a stove (as in the children's nursery) or the provision of unstructured activities in waiting areas. This is the tone of Fourier's prescriptions for the phalanstery, the architecture of "passional attraction" translated from speculation to reality.

"Circulation paths" were a recognizable feature of community architecture; they were places where society members were forced to interact with one another, places where social space could be used to enhance and monitor social interaction. Though it hardly looked like a beehive, the Mansion House operated like one. It has been described as a "machine for communal living," and all the residents' efforts within that home were turned towards perfecting it. The Hawley diary opens rather prosaically with the entry: "I went to WP and finished polishing my pin boxes. I gave Doty a Turkish bath and slept with Haden tonight. Tirzah asked me when I was getting Doty to sleep." Willow Place (WP) was an industrial building about a mile from the main site, and Doty and Haden were young children in his temporary care. At the time of this entry Victor Hawley was thirty-one years old, working in the Dentist Office (D.O.) making impressions for false teeth. Part of the large Hawley family that had joined the colony in the 1850s, he was slight of build (126 pounds), apparently in good health, but still shifting around (or being shifted around) from job to job in order to find his proper niche in the colony. He was not a leading member or someone who stood out as part of the generation who had come of age during an era of colony prosperity—a period unmarked by serious economic or social problems. Noyes had stated in 1868 that one of the reasons why stirpiculture could be introduced was because the society had conquered all the "practical" difficulties associated with building a cooperative society. In addition much of the support for the eugenics scheme came from a portion of the younger generation best represented by Theodore Noyes, whose studies at Yale had introduced him to both Comte and Galton.

There was another side to this generation, and one that too little has been made of: they were the children of affluence, a generation who had witnessed an accommodation take place between the world and Oneida. That adjustment had been a gradual one, one developed because of increased business and social contacts over the years, university training for some young adults, music lessons in New York for others. It is not that they were, as a group, spoiled or irreligious for that characterization would suggest too sharp a break with their religious past, but that this new generation had exercised greater choices, known prosperity, and was removed both physically and psychologically from the early history of the society, with its persecutions and its peculiar and special sense of its mission to the world.

Constance Noyes Robertson, in her *Oneida Community: An Autobiography, 1851–1876,* asserts that this second generation had "lost faith," and when they lost it "they began to lose everything—their security, their agreement, their selfishness, their happiness." When John H. Noyes withdrew from the leadership position in April 1876 he, according to Robertson, created a void that could not be filled, and his son Theodore "strove earnestly to fill the void with all sorts of new theories, new panaceas, new regimens, from Darwinism and evolution to spiritualism and hot baths." What Robertson failed to see was that these "panaceas" were an integral part of the 1860s and 1870s and that these ideas resonated with some members of the younger generation. They were not mere exotic filling put in to plug a void but represented some of the major intellectual and social tendencies of the day. Victor Hawley's passion for collecting butterflies, for example, was a part of this new scientific spirit. More important, however, was his desire to exercise choice over his personal life and to explore a world of sentiment and love that Oneida forbade.

From his diary we learn that one of Hawley's tasks throughout this period was to sleep with community children and to care for them in the evening. Child care in the community was a collective enterprise, with children sleeping in a section of the Mansion House. The "Children's Department" was housed in a wing of the Mansion House built in 1869–1870 and linked to the main building by passages in every story. Between 1870 and 1876 the department became the center of the colony's new vision and hope. By 1874 there were fifty children under twelve years old living there under the care of a staff of six (one man, five women). Mothers kept their children in their own quarters until they were fourteen or fifteen months old and then passed them into the care of the department. Initially, children were placed in the East Room, where "they have their play things, their picture books, blocks, wheels, toys, etc. There the other children came to play with them when permitted, there the other babies came when their mother want to take them a-pleasuring. There the fathers came to see them, particularly after dinner, and there the mothers came at any hour."

Mothers could take their children away for an hour or so and fathers could visit, but the children were returned to the care of the children's department. In the evening the babies slept with adults in different rooms. Children became at this age true "community children," and their world was the world of the nursery, with its professional staff. This "corps"—as *The Circular* referred to them—were not on duty all the time but had limited care over the children. "Their care does not include the wants of the children. They attend them at the table, but have nothing to do with the preparation of their

food. They dress them but do not have to mend their clothes."
When the children were ready for school, they were taught by
other community members, and when old enough to work, the
children were supervised by members at the work place:
"Those who keep the Children's House have it for their care to
make it good, to mold their habits, to know where they are,
and go in and out with them, giving them all suitable change
and amusement and attending to every little incidental
want."

In her memoir about her childhood at Oneida, Corinna
Ackley Noyes recalled only beautiful and tender memories.
"As I look back on those days, I am impressed with the
amount of time, thought and ingenuity the children's welfare
commands from men and women alike. The rearing of
healthy, happy children was a major enterprise in the Oneida
Community." At the age of six or seven they graduated from
the East Room to the South Room, a larger room that gave
them more freedom. Both rooms were furnished with a "sensi-
ble austerity" but contained all that the children needed to
occupy them. "For readers there was a bookcase filled with
children's books and on dull days some house mother or father, noting mounting restlessness would read some story
aloud." For other children there were blocks to engage their
abilities, but to Noyes's mind the outstanding feature of the
South Room was an engraving that depicted the tragic journey of Christian in *Pilgrim's Progress*. "I don't remember who
first read us the story and pointed out the vicissitudes Christian encountered, but it preached a powerful sermon and
brought us the idea of warfare with sin very early—too early,
I think." Despite her misgivings about the heavy atmosphere
of morality that hung over the room, her memories were of a
caring and warm environment where attention to the physical, social, and moral development of each child was manifest.

Despite the existence of this separate facility, children—
particularly in the 1870s—were so omnipresent that, beginning in 1871, a "Children's Hour" was introduced into the
community schedule. "Various persons about the house are
engaged to take a child an hour in the evening, doing their
best in the time to instruct and amuse him . . . . So when six

o'clock comes, the children scatter to the rooms to which they are invited,where they stay until seven. They go to the same rooms for a week and then pass on to others."

All this was done to enhance the social environment both for the children and for other community members; yet the colony remained on guard against not only special attachments to biological parents but "possessiveness" in any form. In March 1874 *The Circular* urged that the managers of the Children's House and the "whole family" should look into the matter of "petting" small children. "It is very common for certain persons, and had been for many, to take possession of babies when they just begin to act prettily and make idols of them." This spirit ("soaking in special love") was dangerous because it took away from the general community spirit and emphasized an "exclusive" and "idolatrous" relationship. All in all there were a total of seven rooms set aside for the children who, as they got older, were allowed to wander freely into other areas of the community.

Victor's care of the children seems a part of his regular routine, though he was not apparently assigned to the Children's Department but to the Dentist's Office. Within a few days of that first entry he is transferred out of that office to the "Villa" (the first Mansion House), where he works as a stocker. "I told her (Tirzah Miller) that W. W (William Woolworth) said that they thought I was not adapted to my business and that they were not geting the full benefit of my capabilities." This shifting around from job to job continues throughout the diary years and represents both Hawley's inability to find a suitable job at Oneida and the colony's own commitment to job rotation. What Victor desires more than anything else at this point is to settle into a routine, and that routine involves him in more than just a regular job; it involves a settled relationship with Mary Jones.

His separation from her had been mandated by the colony because they had established an "exclusive" relationship. His intermediary with her is Tirzah Miller, John Humphrey Noyes's confidante, through whom he must make all overtures. In conversation with her that day he asks if he "could have some talk with Mary as I had spoken to her only once for two months and 8 days." His request is granted, and he gets a half-hour with her. As a result he feels "far better," then notes in the diary "she slept 2 ½ hours here last night." Strong measures were usually taken at Oneida to break up "exclusive" relationships: individuals were subjected to criticism sessions and, in extreme cases, physically separated, with one partner sent off to another colony center, usually Wallingford, Connecticut, later referred to as the "penùl colony."

The first hint in the diary that his desire to have a child with Mary Jones was a strong one comes when he records the following conversation: "Mrs. Dunn has some good talk with me and said that she did not think a combination was good between us to have a baby as Mary's mind was affected. I gave her my views and my reasons for thinking that she would have a strong baby, that her mother, sisters second baby were strong and healthy." During 1876 the stirpiculture plan was still in effect, but there was growing concern about its effect on colony life. Theodore Noyes's emphasis upon a "scientific" criterion for mating and John H. Noyes's insistence on a spiritual standard had created a controversy that could be resolved only by pseudo-scientific methods. Of the fifty-one applicants who applied to have children, forty-two were approved and nine denied on the grounds that they were "unfit." Mary's unfitness was twofold: her mind was "affected," and she was thought "too sickly" to have a child. The affliction that gripped her mind was her "excessive desire to have a child." When the diary begins, the selection process is still in the hands of the twelve-member "Stirpiculture Committee," headed by Theodore Noyes; the power to sanction a combination shifts back to a central committee of elders in March and April 1876.

Victor Hawley had been criticized in the fall of 1875 for getting into too "close" a relationship with Mary, and they had been instructed to separate for two months. After that period of separation they are reunited in early January. Mary and Victor begin to visit one another. "Mary came to the tower after dinner and sat on my lap . . . " but they refrain from sexual contact. Late in January they meet again, and he records their meeting. "Mary came after dinner today feeling bad from the talk and we made special love last night. I cheered up and she felt better after meeting. We pray God give us a baby."

His "special love" with her not only violated colony practice but had placed them in line for serious censure. Oddly enough, the word *special* is an archaic term for *paramour* and paramour she had become to him. She was now his reason for being, his primary and exclusive love, and they had gone well beyond the bounds of acceptable community behavior. Now, all they can do is wait.

His diary then returns to the normal rounds of his day, focusing particularly on his care of other community children. "Mrs Kelly takes care of Phoebe the forepart of the night and calls me at two tomorrow night" (February 7, 1876). Among his other concerns is his hobby of insect collecting. As an amateur entomologist he regularly collected and mounted specimens and was, like others of his generation, interested in science. On the one hand he shows a strong bent towards scientific investigation and research, and on the other, an inclination toward his work as a dental technician. He is clearly unsure just what he ought to be doing with his life. "Edson spoke to me this morning about going into the Job P [rinting] Office to fill Milford's place. A committee of W. A. Hinds, W. H. W., W. G. Allen and Tirzah and Martha. W. A. H. thought I ought to quit the insect business. The others said I had better give it but little attention Martha said the committee was to advise and help me." In short, he has been given a strong warning that his interest in insect collecting is not one that the community approves of because he has become too obsessed with it. Yet the tradition at Oneida was to offer constructive criticism, and the committee does just that and limits itself to giving (as he records it) "advice and help."

Neither advice nor help was ever wanting at Oneida, and the fine line that separated an order from "advice" was not always easy to discern. Members' belief in constant criticism kept up the social pressure on all of them and forced them to be self-critical about behavior. When Victor reflected in his diary on the session, he wrote: "I thought it not very comforting advice" and as the result "slept for an three-fourths of an hour." Criticism sessions were never comfortable in any sense and represented the hardest part of community life according to all comentators. Their "faults" were told to them during these sessions and sometimes published in the community press. At other times individuals were the subject of communitywide discussion during a general meeting.

In 1873, for example, during the week between Christmas and New Year, the elder Noyes suggested that all work stop and that the community engage in a series of mutual criticisms. A standard criticism (this one requested by a member) appeared in the *Daily Journal* of April 14, 1863. A "Mr H." was criticized for his "penchant for taking on the spirit of the world while out peddling; for too much freedom of communication with outsiders in relation to our social matters . . . for hardness of spirit and an itching to get out of shop." Criticisms also contained positive statements—called "commendatory criticism"—intended to bolster morale and provide a balanced view of a member. Other sessions were leveled at "groups" who exhibited certain tendencies, as in 1874, when there was a report on the "prima donna fever" apparent in one of the young women; this was used to point out that it was a "fault" in many others like her. This "evil" had seized those for whom "music had evidently become a selfish, personal thing; they look on their talents, their reputation, their ability and success in music as their own." One of the sources of the problem lay in the fact that the colony had lately gotten its music "from the world, and had gone to New York for musical education, and we are suffering the consequences."

Victor took the criticism in stride, accepted his job reassignment, and began his work in the printing office. Mary Jones, not the *American Socialist* (the colony journal), was still at the center of his life. "Last night Mary came up to the tower and lay down in bed with me after I had gone to bed and where we both cuddled up more than ever. We have had to wait so long and have been without communication for three months that the greatest of love was strong between us." *Communication* is the term used at times in the diary to describe sexual relations.

Victor's use of particular terms to describe sexual relations comes from the common language of discourse at

Oneida; yet it was also flavored by the prevailing philosophy of the stirpiculture experiment. Words like *connection, start, expose, communication,* and *service* all have had varied etymologies. Some were taken from the language of animal breeding and represented the argot of horse culture, but there are other social and psychological sources at work in the usage of the words. They reflect the language of domestication and submission, the language of utility, and the language of master and servant relationships. By the 1870s some of the terms—such as *communication* to mean "sexual intercourse"—were no longer in common usage, and the term, in fact, never had wide currency, though Smollett used it in *Humphrey Clinker* (1793) to describe how a physician at Bath who had cured a prostitute had "communicated with her three times—I always ascertain my cures in that manner." To have *connection* appears in the diary in much the same context as *communication.* It was an American adaptation of the word *connexion* and was first used in this sexual context by Boswell in 1791 to describe illicit sexual relations.

John Humphrey Noyes had used both terms in his 1848 publication, *Bible Communism* (Oneida, 1848). In describing the sequence of events leading him to the "discovery" of male continence he emphasized that one of his prime motivations had been to avoid any more premature births for his wife. She had had five births, with four leading to premature deliveries and the loss of a child four times. "This experience was what directed my studies and kept me studying. After our last disappointment, I pledged my word to my wife that I would never again expose her to such fruitless suffering." In Noyes's case he believed that the pregnancies had resulted in pain and anguish for his wife, Harriet Holton. Oneida had hoped (as a community) to eliminate what it called the "propagative" and elevate the "amative."

For Noyes sexual intercourse was a means to a social and religious end and not to a physical one. In the sexual act there were several elements: the "conjunction of the organs of union. . . . the interchange of magnetic influences, or conversation of spirits through the medium of that conjunction." Ordinary sexual intercourse (as performed in the world) was, for

Noyes, "a momentary affair, terminating in exhaustion and disgust." Children were a means to a higher end, certainly not an end in themselves.

For Victor Hawley and Mary Jones to be "exposed" carried with it great risks, but exhaustion and disgust do not seem to have been uppermost in their minds. It did, however, lay them open to other meanings implicit in the word itself since they could be deprived of shelter, expelled to another country, left unprotected from hostile elements—all appropriate definitions of the word *expose*.

Two of the terms that were used in the diary in connection with sexual relations were borrowed explicitly from the language of animal breeding: *started* and *service*. In his *Essay on Scientific Propagation* (Oneida, 1877) Noyes had drawn heavily on the literature of plant and animal breeding, which led him to conclusion that "the positive good of the process is carried on by selecting for propagation the best individuals of both sexes, but especially males" (14). Men as well as stallions could impregnate an infinite number of females, but since women were limited to one child per nine-month period, it was obvious who should take the lead. "Thus the present generation of fine horses in this country, number probably in the millions, is said to have come mainly from less than a dozen famous stallions" (15). He believed that the science of breeding showed that in an attempt to create a "new race" it had been necessary to select a "new Adam and Eve," and "breed in and in." Success required, not just breeding selected pairs, but the recognition that certain blood lines, or families, were clearly superior and that the best results could be obtained by managing the pairings. "Finally there can be no doubt that by segregating superior families, and by breeding them in and in, superior varieties of human beings might be produced which would be comparable to the thoroughbreds in all the domestic races" (21).

The institution of marriage was an "absolute bar" to scientific propagation because it distributed the business of births to animal instincts in a "wild state," with the result that we have a "general scramble" rather than careful mating. Marriage created an additional bar because it operated under a set of legal restrictions (incest statutes) that prevent close family breeding.

Having set out the theory, Noyes then described its boundaries and limitations. "In the first place," he wrote, "they might not lessen human liberty" nor "injure HOME." In his defense of both liberty and home he was echoing the conventional sentiments of nineteenth-century America, but Oneida's definition of both terms was certainly at odds with the prevailing one. Mating could be brought about without "regard to the sentimental specialties that now control it," and it could be done for those whose liberty consisted of following "rational laws" because they loved "truth more than sentimentality" (31).

Victor Hawley refused to be domesticated, to give up that sentimental illusion that he could have a special love. Oneida, with the stirpiculture plan, tried to control its members within the bounds of laws that were both man-made and God-given. The Darwinian law had postulated, they believed, a new science, and Francis Galton with his essay on the "First Step Towards the Domestication of Animals," which first appeared in *Macmillans* magazine, and his book *Hereditary Genius* (London, 1869) had shown the way. But such a plan and the way it functioned at Oneida led in the direction of crushing the spirit of individualism and bringing to heel rampant passion. Though the experiment was begun in 1869, it had its roots in Noyes's long-standing fears that sexuality had to be conquered, that the flesh had to be brought under the law, and that he and the members of his family should take the lead.

When Erastus Hamilton spoke of the Hawley family getting into the stirpiculture plan he was talking about them not only as believers who had roots in the Perfectionist faith, but also as a biological cohort that could be combined with other cohorts. Here was a shaky scientific and religious marriage that was, in the long run, doomed to failure. Noyes, in his *Essay on Scientific Propagation,* cited the work of W. H. H. Murray, whose *The Perfect Horse* (London, 1873) outlined some general principles about breeding and, at times, extended the discussion to include the human species. In it there is a defense of the practice of "breeding in and in," with specific reference to its appropriateness for the human race. "In reference to this matter of in-breeding, I am inclined to think that not only should it be done with profit in the case of blood relations." Murray acknowledged that the implications of these "incestuous" unions were complex and fraught with difficulty, but he argued "the world began with a single pair; and in the human family, inbreeding and that, too, of the closest kind must have been the rule. Who can doubt but that the perfect produced the perfect?"

According to Murray the Jews maintained themselves by intermarriage, and when one looked at the hardy lines produced by the English nobility one saw a movement from strength to strength. There were cautions, of course, that had to be observed in such delicate unions, particularly when the inbreeding was close: "if both parents be vicious, then will the foal be sure to be an ugly brute anyway." "Outcrossing"—in the case of horses—might be allowed if there was breeding back to the superior stock. Temperament played an important role in all this selection process and was, in fact, more important than the physical characteristics of the mated pair. "The amount of flesh does not decide the character of spiritual essences, and of those subtle forces that make life virile" (143–44).

Noyes drew on not only Darwin and Galton but also writers like Murray to direct his stirpiculture plan. Murray had, for example, warned that under no circumstances should one ever breed a "vicious mare" but only a mare that would be guaranteed to produce a horse that would have all the desired characteristics: docility, endurance, speed, and beauty. Although Noyes was not one to make such a crude analogy, one can only speculate on his response to Murray's ideal horse—the Morgan. Noyes himself was almost a parallel to John Morgan, the Massachusetts-born, Vermont-raised stallion that had contributed through his line "more than any other animal had to the wealth of the United States." For strength, for durability, for temperament there had never been anything like him, though many said that the breed was "too small, too small." John Morgan had been able to "transmit his own likeness to his descendants" and gave that power "to his sons." It was through that line that this perfect horse had made his contribution. When crossed with twenty other horse families he "dominated over them all. No matter what the dam might be the colt was sure to look like the sire" (294).

Short, Vermont-born and -reared, John Humphrey Noyes could hardly not have identified with the Morgan line. There was constant talk in the community about the "Noyes look and temperament" and about the tendency of the Noyes stock toward spiritual things. The sense of family identification, of racial pride is evident in all his writings from the *Berean* to the *Essay on Scientific Propagation*. John Morgan had sired thoroughbreds over all New England; John Humphrey Noyes, through the stirpiculture plan, was going to do the same. The Noyes family, the Hawley family, and the Jones family, each with their distinctive racial characteristics, were part of the plan. Racial and psychological traits drawn from close observation and from an intimate knowledge of blood lines were to be matched, to be bred and, if the future appeared good, were to be rebred.

The Hawley, Jones, and Noyes families all had some contribution to make to the grand experiment; they all had different roles within a hierarchy. Men were superior to women in what they could bring to a union; the Noyeses were (as a family) superior to others because of their genetic stuff and their biblical line (the line of Moses as it were). The Hawleys and Joneses (as families) were probably at the same level, though clearly not perfect stock, when one considers that Mary Jones's father, William, was deaf and had never participated in the colony social practices because he was prone to epileptic fits. But there were other considerations—human ones—that were brought into play during the selection process: a willingness to be put into "service," an attitude of compliance toward community preference, and, of course, a desire to satisfy everyone. Yet not everyone was to be satisfied, as both Mary Jones and Victor Hawley painfully learned.

When the time came to set up the selection process the elder Noyes spoke approvingly of the words of Charles Wylls Eliot, whose article on breeding had appeared in the *Galaxy* magazine in 1869. "At this moment ten times as much care and thought and money are devoted to the production of perfect horses or pigs, as to men and women." Eliot noted that the world was full of "weedy, homely, suffering human beings," but he believed that a man could be as handsome as a pig, and a woman's beauty on a par with the beauty of a horse. The animal similes were never far from the surface at Oneida. Clearly, the language of coupling, with its "starts," its "connections," its "exposing" were both of the barnyard and of the gospel enclosure.

Mary was in turmoil because the colony had failed to obtain a headstone for her stillborn child, and the child's death in 1872 was clearly still on her mind. The community's failure to memorialize the child stands in her mind as a conscious rebuff. Symbolically, the headstone stands for her living desire for her child, and the community's refusal to erect one in a timely fashion suggests that it wished to repress both the memory of the child and the woman who bore it. Both, in the community's eyes, are dead; both, mistakes; both, sickly. Early in March she comes to Victor with some good news. "There were a number of people trying." Apparently, the ban on sexual liaisons leading toward conception had been lifted by the Stirpiculture Committee, and that decision renewed their hopes for a child of their own. Immediately, Mary makes an approach to William Woolworth, a colony elder and member of the committee, and asks "if we could have a baby." Woolworth responded by saying that he would bring her request before the board.

According to Constance Noyes Robertson the selection of partners had passed back into the hands of the elders during March and April. At this time there was also considerable discussion about both Theodore Noyes's spiritual values and his ability to lead the society. Still, it was his father's wish that he take the helm, and in April 1876 Noyes resigned in favor of his son.

Mary tried to further their case by approaching Charlotte Thayer, another committee member. "Mary talked with Mrs Thayer and said she saw that we were promised that we might be among the first to commence trying again and that there were a number that were trying, but still Mrs. Thayer could give no assurances." In one of the few almost illegible sentences in the diary Victor records a conversation with his brothers Alfred and Roswell, who try to convince him that someone else should have a child by Mary Jones. Victor seems to waver: "I told him I could give up Mary if it was necessary." Fortunately, that conversation was so powerful for Victor that he recorded it in another journal book he kept (mainly for supply purchases). "Alfred Roswell talked to me after meeting and said I could not have a baby by Mary that the family did not sympathize with our having one and that we could not have one for five years I said I could give her up if necessary the next day."

There are two ways to look at the entry: first, that the brothers were jealous of the liaison, and second, that Victor was still willing to submit to community criticism and advice. He appeared at that point willing to give Mary up for the greater good of the society. Later, the rivalry among the brothers broke out into open hostility, but for the moment they are still supportive of one another.

The society was being torn apart by the stirpiculture experiment despite the rhetoric of group solidarity. In a letter to Dr. Anita Newcomb McGee, an anthropologist who later wrote about the experiment, James Towner gave (in succinct fashion) his thoughts about the causes of dissension at this time.

> Dissent began to show itself openly in 1876 when Mr. N. undertook to make and instal as his successor in leadership his son, Dr. T. R. Noyes, in many respects as able a man as his father, but who had been to Yale and graduated, and came from there Positivist, an unbeliever in the religion upon which the community was founded. From this it gradually extended to other things ; the chief trouble arising among the second generation, in rebelling at some things in the administration of the system of complex marriage" (James Towner to Anita N. McGee, November 1, 1894).

A few days after his conversation with his brothers Victor has an encouraging conversation with Tirzah Miller about his prospects, but finds that his older brother is still urging him to yield to the community and accept its guidance. Alfred sends him a note. "Roswell and I hope that you will not go directly to Mary and try to arrange the matter between yourselves, but go to Mr. Woolworth and let him help you. You will then be more sure of starting right & of having the community & a good spirit to back you."

Victor's answer to Alfred reflects his continuing desire to have a child by one and only one woman. "I wrote to him declining to do so." In his business account book he recorded the actual letter sent on March 7. "Dear Brother: I decline going to Mr. Woolworth and making any such statement, or of giving up the idea of having a baby by Mary."

Victor's refusal is a refusal to accept the "community spirit" and to keep his own spirit alive despite community pressure. It is a spirit of independence, a spirit that was, by any Oneida standard, anticommunity. By midnight on Friday, March 10 he had finished a letter to the colony patriarch, John H. Noyes, setting forth his history with Mary and others and stating their joint desire to participate in the experiment:

Dear Father Noyes,
    In 1872 I had the desire of having a child by Mary Jones, but we were called on to try with others. I tried with Jane Abbott but did not succeed. Mary tried with Mr. Seymore and you know the results. She was promised another by him but she was not to have one by him. Last spring it was decided that we might have one but were not permitted to try until the last month before it was decided for all to stop trying. I was told that we might begin again when others did in March. Having heard that others were trying, the other day I asked Mr.Woolworth if we could try again. He said that most of the combinations were started by W.C. Last fall I was criticized for getting in to close relationship with Mary and was advised to separate from her. I did so and did not speak to her for two months & have done the best I know how to give satisfaction by my course. Knowing that Mary would like to have a child by me I would rather have one by her than to have one by someone

who does not wish to have one by me. As you have expressed
some interest in having the Hawley family propagate I will
frankly say that I would like a baby by Mary. Hoping to get
a line from you if you have anything to say.
    Yours in the service of Christ
    R. V. Hawley

Three days later he had his answer from the elder Noyes:

Dear Victor,
    Your presentation of your case is very reasonable &
persuasive & I should be much pleased to have your wishes
gratified. I will send your letter to Mr.Woolworth and you
[SH] Thayer's [SH] J.O. after breakfast may show him this.
Such a matter ought to be decided by the family at O.C
rather than by me. The only hindrance to my full sympathy
with the combination you propose is my remembrance of
Mary's excessive desire for children which always seemed to
me dangerous on account of the liability to disappointment
but probably she has improved & I will certainly do not
wish to object to what seems to you safe and wise.
    Yours truly
    J. H. Noyes

Noyes's deferential and generally supportive letter is a
letter written by a man caught in the middle of contending
forces and parties. His own withdrawal from the leadership at
Oneida had created a vacuum, and he had no desire to fill it
again, even though there was a clear need to do so. Noyes's
desire to "gratify" Victor's wish is carefully balanced against
the need to keep the political lines straight.
    For the first time in the diary Victor and Mary's personal
history is clearly laid out. During the early years of the stirpiculture plan (it began in 1869) they wanted a child but
"were called on to try with others." His liaison with Jane Abbott failed, and hers with George Seymour led to a stillborn
birth. In spring, 1875, they were promised that they might
"try again"; however, that plan was interrupted by a crisis
during the summer of 1875, when Theodore Noyes's leadership was questioned. So now, almost a year later and after a

period of enforced separation, they want to renew the process they began in 1872.

Since the elder Noyes had sent the decision on to Oneida, Victor must now contend with the local leadership, albeit a shifting one. On March 13 he turns Noyes's note over to William Woolworth and receives, in turn, a discouraging reply. "I think folks here think & feel very much as Mr.Noyes does about it. They would like to have you gratified, and yet the inordinate and unsanctified desire especially on Mary's particular, make folks hesitate and shrink from the consequences." The problem lay with Mary. For the community her tendency toward "philoprogenitiveness"—the phrenological term for excessive mothering—was too strong, and it branded her as someone so caught up in her own "unsanctified" desires that she was out of step with colony will, called "community feeling."

Woolworth's response made Mary "downhearted and discouraged," and she talked over the matter with Mr. Seymour and then with Mr. Woolworth. On March 20 Victor recorded (in shorthand) the following entry: "I got Mary to come to bed at 12 and said I must not seek to have communication. I did not ask but did not sleep but a few moments and at 4.15 she said to me 'don't suffer any more' and I did not and came to a crisis and exposed her. We did not feel that we had done wrong for Mary has been promised a baby so many times and then not given a chance to have one." Not only did he come to a "crisis," but he had ejaculated inside her; he had "exposed" her to pregnancy.

Within a week—presumably a week when she believed she was fertile—they make love again. "Mary went to bed with me at about 11 and went home about one. We had communication and I said that it would be easy for me to come to a crisis. She said she wished that I would but I did not." First, masturbation ("used hand"), then intercourse to orgasm, then they hoped, a child of their own. It was not to be a community child. In short, they were "trying"—to use community language—in secret, though their secret could not be such for long.

Even though they were having sexual relations to or-

gasm, Victor continues to press for approval through community channels; he finds that his own family now constitutes a
stumbling block. "I talked with Mr. Hamilton just before
meeting. He said the first he heard about it [their desire to
have a child] was when Alfred Roswell Martha Mrs. Noyes
and Mrs. Dunn came into his room and wanted him to put a
stop to our having a baby as A & R could not Mr. H. said he
hoped there would not be any will about it on either side &
that we would wait on God." Mary and Victor had chosen not
to wait on God (for inspiration and guidance), and their secret
would be short-lived. Opposition to their union was mounting,
and on April 1 the Stirpiculture Committee met and gave
their answer. "The committee decidedly disapprove of our
having a baby."

For Victor the next few weeks were ones of profound melancholy and despair compounded by illness. He takes to his
bed, and the journal is full of brooding thoughts about Oneida
and his own future at the colony. "I said I thought I should be
happier away from here and that I had been strongly tempted
to go"; "I sent for Frederic this morning and whilst telling
how I had been tempted to stay with Mary because folks were
watching us and that if I went it would spoil our chance of
having a baby." By April 5, however, their secret is out because William Woolworth came to him with the news that
Mary had confessed about his having "exposed" her. This
news drives him back to his bed, and he takes his breakfast
delivered to his room. At Oneida sickness and sin were twin
aspects of the same disease—unbelief. His physical condition
is a mirror image of his spiritual state; he has grown weak in
the flesh and failed to strengthen himself against this attack
of anticommunity spirit. By retreating to his bed Victor has
confirmed by default his fall from grace. Overtaken by sin
and selfishness, he is now laid low by illness.

Once discovered, he now seeks the community's forgiveness. In a letter to an Oneida elder, Erastus Hamilton, he
pleads, "I asked God and the community's forgiveness." During the following week the full weight of colony and family
censure fall on him. His father arrives from Wallingford, and
the Hawley family meets with Oneida's leading figures for a

criticism session. During that session with elders E. H. Hamilton, Mrs. Noyes, and Mrs. Dunn, Victor learns that there is little chance that Mary Jones will ever be allowed to have a child. But his thoughts remain with Mary and the possibility of her pregnancy. "I feel as if life were weary here & all that kept me was the thought that Mary might be with child and I ought to stay and help support it." His sense of personal obligation to her is obvious, though she was not at risk of being abandoned by the colony since they would have assumed responsibility for any child born. Emotionally, he remains commited to her, though there is evidence that she feels less attached to him.

His physical or psychosomatic illness continues. He has dizzy spells and cramps in the hands and legs and finally, a full fainting spell. Invited by his father to go to Wallingford for a few weeks (presumably to take his mind off Mary), Victor finds that the plans have all changed suddenly, and for the worse. "I was not going but Mary was to have a baby by Mr. Leonard." "Leonard" refers to either Stephen or John Leonard, two brothers who had come into the society in 1848. Stephen was fifty-six and John fifty-three in 1876. Victor has been dealt a double blow: first, he was denied his role as lover, and now, he is to be denied a role as a father. Depression floods over him, and he confides in his journal: "I am weak in every bone I can hardly crawl around. Anxious to see Mary they let her come to my room about 6pm for ¾ of an hour. Her presence gave me new life & strength which lasted all night & freedom from a haid cold & pressure in my head."

There is no indication of Mary's feelings about Mr. Leonard, but clearly, she has bowed to community sentiment and decided to have a child by an elder leader.

> She said she told Mr. H she could keep me in the community & that she would stick to the community but she still loved me the same as ever. She wanted to go away dreadfully. Saturday I did too when Emma said she was unwell I felt as if I could go & almost leave her to escape the trouble to come, I gave her a cologne bottle and orange and lock of hair. Parted with good feelings and love for those happy moments & I tried to keep bright for her sake.

With Mary's departure to Wallingford the first section of the diary comes to a close. During these intense three months Victor has used his diary for solace and comfort. Clearly, the community still exerts enormous influence over them both, and he feels both resentment and frustration. His violation of colony practice has been punished, his lover has been banished to another colony to have a child by another man, and his own life seems to be ebbing away. His diary notation for April 12 is a melancholy one. "A dreary forenoon, out of doors till 11.30 F. Marks came to my room I told him how I felt. I had a spasm about 12.30 and life seemed nearly ended for a few minutes." The choices open to him at this juncture are few: he can either leave the colony and strike out on his own, accept the colony ruling and return to the fold, or continue to hope (as he does) that he and Mary will be united again.

The Diary of Victor Hawley
January 1, 1876–April 11, 1876

Saturday January 1 1876
I went to WP and finished polishing my pin boxes. I gave Doty a Turkish bath & sleep with Haden tonight. Tirzah asked me when I was getting Doty to sleep

Sunday January 2 1876
I had a few minutes talk with Mr. Woolworth this morning who said they were going to take me out of the Dentist Office as soon as they could get a place for me. I wrote to Mary this evening to come to the Tower as Roswell was gone. I sat up till two but she did not come.

Monday January 3 1876
Edson came into the Dentist Office this forenoon and told me I was going to work in Otis place at the Villa as stocker and I only slept an hour last night.

Tuesday January 4 1876
I had some talk with Tirzah this morning at the Villa. She was surprised to learn that I was out of the D Office. I told her that WHW said that they thought I was not adapted

to my business and that they were not getting the full benefit of my capabilities   I asked her if I could have some talk with Mary as I had spoken to her only once for two months and 8 days. I had a ½ hour talk with Mary after dinner and feel far better. She slept 2½ hours here last night.

Wednesday January 5 1876

Mary came to my room after dinner and say on my lap. Tirzah had not said anything to Mrs. Dunn.

Thursday January 6 1876

Mrs. Dunn had some good talk with me and said she did not think a combination was good between us to have a baby as Mary's mind was affected. I gave her my views and my reasons for thinking that she would have a strong baby, that her mother and sister's second babies were strong and healthy.

Saturday January 8 1876

Mary came to the Villa this morning and I had a few minutes talk with her in my room after Otis looked in the Alarm room, after which Chloe came and asked me if Mrs. Dunn or Mr. W had given us permission to talk. I told her Mrs. Dunn had. Chloe said she did not know but that we were doing it secretly.

Mary came to my room after dinner in the tower, indignant because Chloe was so suspicious and I felt so too but thought it better that it should come so than in an underhanded way.

Sunday January 9 1876

Mary came to the tower after dinner and sat on my lap. I had some talk with Tirzah this evening in regard to my experience.

Monday January 10 1876

The same today. A note from Mrs. Woolworth and I wrote an answer in the evening

Tuesday January 11, 1876
I showed my note to Mary and Mrs. Woolworth's note puts a stop to all talk of stirpiculture and Mary and I went apart again
I am at work naming the birds nests in the bird room.

Friday January 14 1876
Cornelius and I have been getting ready for the Maskurade dance. We worked in his room at the Seminary garret. Roswell had some talk with me and Mary. He thought we had had similar experiences and that Martha thought we were going together too soon. I told Mary and she felt bad and we had some talk after dinner. Roswell and Orrin came up and found the door locked and went downstairs but afterwards someone tried the door and ran downstairs.

Saturday January 15 1876
Preparing for the Masquerade dance   Mary came into the tower after dinner and I cracked some nuts. I sleep with Doty tonight came from the Villa since meeting. Mary came in and sat on my lap for a little while She sleeps in the tower alone tonight and she seems better.

Wednesday January 19 1876
Cornelius is mounting some California birds and I come from the Villa at 10, 11, or 12 o'clock as the work happens to be and work with Cornelius. I am naming the birds nests

Friday January 21 1876
Mary has come to my room in the tower for after dinner
I made some curved strips to hold the window curtains

Saturday January 22 1876
I did not have the chance to speak to Mary today
I put up the strips in Philenas room and in Henry Hunter's room at the Villa

Sunday January 23 1876
Mary came after dinner today feeling bad from the talk and special love last night. I cheered her up and she felt bet-

ter after meeting. We pray God give us a baby. I saw Mary a few minutes after the meeting. She went to the kitchen and I looked for the Villa milk can but it had gone.

Monday January 31 1876
Mary has got so she feels quite well now and does a hard days work whenever called on. I see her most every day when I am over to OC after dinner. I go to the Villa between 5 and 7.30 P.M.

Wednesday February 2 1876
Commenced moving to O.C. from the Villa   I sent over some apples and potatoes by Mr. Geoff

Thursday February 3 1876
A few more things were taken by Mr. Geoff to day

Friday February 4 1876
Moving in good earnest to day. Clarence and I were up early taking up carpets and keeping Lorenzo going with a team. I did not go to O.C. today. Clarence had an examination after dinner in Geometry

Saturday February 5 1876
All the folks were ready to go to O.C. at 5 P.M.

Sunday February 6 1876
Clarence and I went over after meeting & slept at the Villa. The last load of goods moved over this morning

Monday February 7 1876
Mrs. Kelly takes care of Phebe the forepart of the night and calls me at two tomorrow morning.
Clarence and I slept at the Villa last night for the last time Mr. Holt moved in today and Mrs. Sears, Mrs. Lake land and I went to the Villa for some furniture

Tuesday February 8 1876
I sleep with Doty tonight.

Wednesday February 9 1876
Mary came in and talked with me. I went out of the room.
Mary Velzer who had come to the door before me as I was
going back and said she could not find a place to sleep and
wanted to go to her room but told her that someone was in it
while I was gone and she said Orrin was in my bed so she
would find another place to sleep. Mary went into a reception
room and came back after awhile and finally went to bed and
stayed with me.

Monday February 14 1876
Helped Alfred make measurements for a 2 inch steam
pipe through the upper part of the house to the North Wing &
Tower.

Tuesday February 15 1876
[Erasure]
Made out the cost of pipe and covering it & c about
$2.25,00

Wednesday February 16 1876
Edson spoke to me this morning about going into the Job
P. Office to fill Milfords place A committee of W.A. Hinds
W.H.W. W.G Allen, Tirzah and Martha. W.A.H. thought I
ought to quit the insect business. The others said I had better
give it but little attention but Martha said the Committee
was to advise and help me

Thursday February 17 1876
I thought it was not very comforting advice after trying to
look on the bright side for when Edson spoke of the advan-
tages of learning the business I assented and said that I could
print my own labels.
I only slept for an three fourths of an hour

Friday February 18 1876
I helped Mr Shelly fix the pully and weights to the shan-
dleier in the Hall. I slept with Haden in the East Room.

Saturday February 19 1876
A hard days work in the Box Room Edson says.[ ] I worked before breakfast and made 6 ¾ hours for the day.

I slept in the Drawing Room for Lorenzo and Mary came in and we talked till one and we had communication in the chair.

Monday February 21 1876
I commenced work in the Job Printing Office. Setting up letters & lettering cases.

Tuesday February 22 1876
I went to the shop before breakfast after the Dunn Card Press cleaning the press and printing Bill Heads

Wednesday February 23 1876
Printing Silk Envelopes and distributing & cleaning press. Mary came in and lay down with me while Roswell was taking a bath and she comes to my room after dinner and I read from the *Circular*

Thursday February 24 1876
Finished cleaning the Dunn Press and helped make some rollers & c.

Friday February 25 1876
Making rollers & bolting the Dunn press to some joice so as to strengthen the legs for shipping.

Saturday February 26 1876
General overhauling & cleaning in the Job Office by Milford, W. A. Hinds & I. Last night Mary came up to the tower and lay down in the bed with me after I had gone to bed and where we both cuddled up more than ever. We have had to wait so long and have been without communication for three months that the greatest of love was strong between us. I got up at 4:30 A.M. hoping to see her but I did not.

Sunday February 27 1876

H. Malory gave birth to girl at 10:50 last night. Mary and I were in the children's west room till 2 and I used hand. Mary came up to the tower after breakfast. She had a crying time because Mr. Bradley wrote to Mr. Abbott saying that he did not tell Mary she might have a stone for her baby's grave but Mary says that he came to her twice when she was at WC offering to write to Mr. Abbott and have hm cut a stone. She told Carrie M not to do anything to it in the Finance Committee.

Friday March 3 1976

Mary came to the Press Room at 11 AM and asked me to come to the house. I did so. She was told by Minerva that there were a number of people trying. I went to Mr. W H W room and asked if we could have a baby. He said he would bring it before the committee.

Saturday March 4 1876

Mary talked with Mrs. Thayer and said she saw that we were promised that we might be among the first to commence trying again and that there were a number that were trying. Charlotte Maria Thayer and Buelah were trying and they were younger than us. Mrs. Thayer said she was not given such a promise and that she was criticizing Mr. Noyes.

Monday March 6 1876

Alfred and Roswell talked with me after meeting about giving . . . having a baby by Mary . . . I told him I could give up Mary if it was necessary.

Tuesday March 7 1876

I talked with Tirzah about Alfred's and Roswell's talking so to me and she talked quite encouragingly to me and said write to Mr. Noyes. A note from Alfred telling me to go to Mrs. Woolworth to give up Mary. After talking with Tirzah I wrote to him declining to do so.

Wednesday March 8 1876
I slept with Doty.
I got up at five o'clock and commenced a letter to Mr. Noyes about being taken out of the Dentist Office &c

Thursday March 9 1876
I was waiting in the Job Office before breakfast this morning and Mrs. Woolworth and Mr. Hinds came through

Friday March 10 1876
I finished my letter to Mr. Noyes at 12 P.M. I received the following note from A the 7th

March 7, 1876

Dear Victor,
Roswell and I hope that you will not go directly to Mary and try to arrange the matter between yourselves, but go to Mr. Woolworth and let him help you. You will then be more sure of starting right & having the community & a good spirit to back you.
Your brother,
Alfred
OC March 10, 1876

Dear Father Noyes,
In 1872 I had the desire of having a child by Mary Jones, but we were called on to try with others. I tried with Jane Abbott but did not succeed. Mary tried with Mr. Seymore and you know the results. She was promised another by him but afterwards it was decided that she was not to have one by him. Last spring it was decided that we might have one but were not permitted to try until the last month before it was decided for all to stop trying. I was told that we might begin again when others did in March. Having heard that others were trying, the other day I asked Mr. Woolworth if we could try again. He said that most of the combinations were started by W.C. Last fall I was criticized for getting into too close relations with Mary and was advised to seperate from her. I did so and did not speak to her for two months & have done

the best I know how to to give satisfaction by my course. Knowing that Mary would like to have a child by me I had rather have one by her than to have one by someone who does not wish to have one by me. As you have expressed some interest in having the Hawley family propagate I will frankly say that I would like a baby by Mary. Hoping to get a line from you if you have anything to say.

Yours in the service of Christ

R. V. Hawley

WC March 13, 1876

Dear Victor,

Your presentation of your case is very reasonable & persuasive & I should be much pleased to have your wishes gratified. I will send your letter to Mr. Woolworth and you [SH] Thayer's [SH] J.O. after breakfast may show him this. Such a matter ought to be decided by the family at O.C. rather than by me. The only hindrance to my full sympathy with the combination you propose is my remembrance of Mary's excessive desire for children which always seemed to me dangerous on account of the liability to disappointment but probably she has improved & I certainly do not wish to object to what seems to you safe and wise.

Yours Truly,

J. H. Noyes

I showed the letter to Tirzah and handed it to Mr. Woolworth after meeting the 14th next day it was in my box with the following on it.

I think folks here think and feel very much as Mr Noyes does about it. They would like to have you gratified, and yet the inordinate & unsanctified desire especially on Mary's particular, makes folks hesitate & shrink from the consequences.

W. H. W.

I told Mary last night she must not be so down hearted & discouraged. She talked with Mr. Seymour till 12 & sat up till 3. We talked with Mr. Woolworth to day she feels better to night

Sunday March 19 1876

I slept with Doty. Mary Jones was in the Childrens Room to day and Herbert who is # said Aunt Mary what is trouble? She and H. G. Allen explained it to him.

I cracked some walnuts. Mary helped pick out meats. [SH]

Monday March 20 1876

I slept with Haden I got Mary to come to bed about 12 and said I must not seek to have communication. I did not ask but did not sleep but a few minutes and at 4:15 she said to me "do not suffer any more" and I did not and came to a crisis and exposed her. We did not feel that we had done wrong for Mary has been promised a baby so many times and then not given a chance to have one.

Sunday March 26 1876

Mary in Mr. Thayer's room.

Monday March 27 1876

I slept with Doty, and Mary went to bed with me at about 11 and went home about one. We had communication and I said it would be easy for me to come to a crisis. She said she wished that I would but I did not. Tirzah handed me a letter that Mr. Woolworth received from J. H. N. I had a talk with Alfred & Roswell after meeting

Tuesday March 28 1876

I did not sleep but two hours this morning. I was in the reception room till 4:20 this morning.

Wednesday March 29 1876

I talked with Tirzah & she said that she would talk with Mr Hamilton. In the evening she said that Mr Hamilton would talk with me about it.

Thursday March 30 1876

I talked with Mr. Hamilton just before meeting. He said the first he heard about it was Alfred Roswell Martha Mrs. Noyes and Mrs. Dunn came into his room and wanted him to

put a stop to our having a baby as A & R could not. Mr. H.
said he hoped there would not be any will about it on either
side & that we would wait on God.

Friday March 31 1876
I slept with Doty.

Saturday April 1 1876
Mary said that some of the stirpaculteral committee were
spoken to and she thought that they would meet before long. I
found that they met after dinner

Sunday April 2 1876
When Mary went to dinner I found a note from Mr. Woolworth in my box. He said that the committee decidedly disap-
proved of our having a baby. F. Marks came to my room I
showed him my correspondence with Mr. Noyes he said he
would be glad to help me if he could. Mary got me a gem &
cake & strawberry sauce at 11:30 in the Reception Room.

Monday April 3 1876
I have kept my room today Mary talked with Mrs Dunn
& with Fredric she brought up my dinner & Fredric talked
with me after dinner, he asked me if I thought of going away I
said I thought I should be happier away from here and that I
had been strongly tempted to go. He related Abrahams trial
with Isaac & c. I told him there was little hope of happiness as
things had gone here

Tuesday April 4 1876
Tirzah came and said she was dissatisfied with my course
and that I had better go. I asked Mary to go she did not promise me Mr Hamilton & Woolworth talked to me. I went to WP
for 3.75 I put a note in Mr Woolworth box saying that I had
been told that I had better go and I would if clothes and
money were furnished me. I went to Oneida with Alfred I got
a bag shoes rubbers & slips. Martha pleaded to have me stay
& F. Marks also I talked with Mary during meeting in the
Reception Room.

Wednesday April 5 1876

I sent for Fredric this morning and whilst telling how I had been tempted to stay with Mary because folks were watching us and that if I sent it would spoil our chance of having a baby. Mr. Hamilton came up and said Mary had told him about it and how I had exposed her. I told him I had been telling Fredric about it. Mrs Kelley & Emma brought up my breakfast I could only drink some L tea Martha got my dinner Fredric took a letter to Mr. Hamilton I asked God and the communitys forgiveness

Thursday April 6 1876

Father came from W.C. I heard the team drive up and I got up but not in time to see him but he came to my room with Alfred about 8. at 10.30 I went to the sawmill with Fred I felt this A.M. at 9.15 or 10.30 that Mary was going to WC.

Friday April 7 1876

I went to the Job Office to work at 12.30 I felt so bad that I could not work Milford got me some water & Mr Woolworth came & asked to go to a meeting of the Hawley family with E.H. Hamilton Mrs Noyes Mrs Dunn and himself. Mr. Hamilton said there was little or no prospects of Mary's even having a baby. Emma said Mary is unwell to day.

Saturday April 8 1876

I feel as if life was weary here & all that had kept me was the thought that Mary might be with child and I ought to stay & help support it. When coming from the hot room I fell from dizziness or a sudden rush of blood to my head followed by severe cramping in my hands legs and body. F Marks & Mr Towner rubbed me took me into the hot room then out on to a lounge   Father & G. E. C. were called   FM said my face was black from the rush of blood.

Sunday April 9 1876

I feel weak to day too weak to go to the dinning room to my meals, although I have taken only one meal there for a week   I felt strong until to day but have not eaten but little Father took me to ride over west.

Monday April 10 1876

Father and Martha asked me if I would go to WC on a visit of 2 or 3 weeks. I said I would packed my bag & got the rest of my thing in shape so I could send for them if I did not come back. At dinner time Father said I was not going but Mary was to have a baby by Mr. Leonard I asked to sleep with Mary tonight but it was not granted.

Tuesday April 11 1876

I am weak in every bone I can hardly crawl around. Anxious to see Mary they let her come to my room about 6 PM for ¾ of an hour. Her presence gave me new life & strength which lasted all night & freedom from a haid cold & pressure in my head. She said she told Mr H she could keep me in the community & that she would stick to the community but still she loved me same as ever She wanted to go away dreadfully Saturday I did too when Emma said she was unwell I felt as though I could go and almost leave her to escape the trouble to come I gave her a cologne bottle an orange & locks of hair.Parted with good feelings & love for those were happy moments & I tried to keep bright for her sake we eat an orange to gether. I watched the team as it left and the whistle blew for meeting as they disappeared by Goaxes for W.C. with Mary and Father.

1. Victor Hawley.
Courtesy Oneida Community Mansion House.

2. Mary Hawley.
Courtesy Arents Collection, Bird Library, Syracuse University.

3. Hawley family, 1884.
Courtesy Arents Collection, Bird Library, Syracuse University.

4. The diary of Victor Hawley.
Courtesy Arents Collection, Bird Library, Syracuse University.

R. V. Hawley, Entomologist,

ONEIDA COMMUNITY,

ONEIDA, N. Y.

5. Victor Hawley's business journal and card.
Courtesy Arents Collection, Bird Library, Syracuse University.

A lonely day.

JULY,   SUNDAY 29.   1877.

I went up the gulf
after insects I was
out in a heavy rain
& got well soaked

30 I told him that I
might as well go now
as to put it off any
longer and that I
wanted to go & see
Mary he said he told
them I would go to see
her. When they
decided to take me
out of the D.O. He said
I was at liberty to
do as I was a mind to.
Evidently the whole
move & purport of the
meeting was to have us go.

6. Single page diary entry, 1877.
Courtesy Arents Collection, Bird Library, Syracuse University.

A lonely day.

I went up the gulf after insects I was out in a heavy rain & got well soaked

30 I told him that I might as well go now as to put it off any longer and that I wanted to go & see Mary he said he told them I would go to see her when they decided to take me out of the D.O. He said I was at liberty to do as I was a mind to. Evidently the whole move & purport of the meeting was to have us go.

Filling 2 u 2 B. for Martha

A committee of E.H.H. S.S.E. D. L.H.D. G.E.C. Mr Towner, Mrs Loveland, in the South Sitting Room for my benefit. G.E.C. said I had done wrong in giving Phoebe the brandy that Theodore said I ought not to stay in the D.O. Then Mr Towner stated how I stood. E.H.H. said the Community had had forbearance long enough. Mr Towner came to me after meeting & said they had taken me out of the D.O. No other work was given me.

7. Diary entries on facing pages (includes illust. 6), 1877.
Courtesy Arents Collection, Bird Library, Syracuse University.

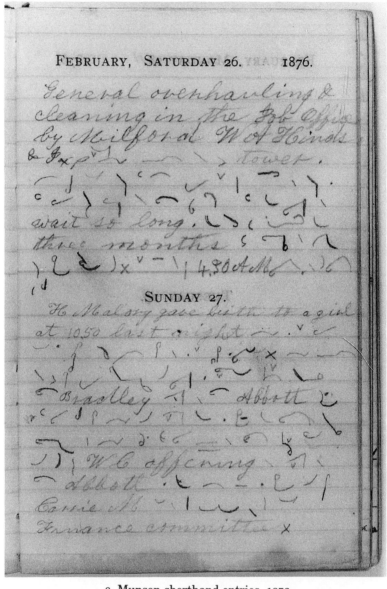

FEBRUARY, SATURDAY 26. 1876.

General overhauling &
cleaning in the Job Office
by Milford W A Hinds
& I. p ... tower.

wait so long.

three months 4.30 AM

SUNDAY 27.

H Mallory gave birth to a girl
at 1050 last night

Bradley ... Abbott

W C offering
Abbott

Carrie M

Finance committee

8. Munson shorthand entries, 1876.
Courtesy Arents Collection, Bird Library, Syracuse University.

MARCH,   MONDAY 27.   1876.

I slept with Doty.

[shorthand]

[shorthand] about 11

[shorthand] about _[shorthand]_

[shorthand]

I _[shorthand]_ wished _[shorthand]_

Tirzah handed me a letter
that Mr Woolworth received
from S H N. I had a talk with
Alfred & Roswell after meeting

TUESDAY 28.

I did not sleep but two hours
this morning I was in the Recepti
on room till 4.20 this morning

MARCH,   WEDNESDAY 29.   1876.

I talked with Tirzah &
she said that she would
talk with Mr Hamilton
In the Evening she said
Mr Hamilton would talk
with me about it

THURSDAY 30.

I talked with Mr Hamil-
ton just before meeting
He said the first he heard
about it was Alfred Roswell
Martha Mrs Noyes & Mrs Dunn
came into his room
and wanted him to put a stop
to our having a baby as A & B
could not. Mr H said he hoped
there would not be any will
about it on either side & that

9. Shorthand diary entries, 1876.
Courtesy Arents Collection, Bird Library, Syracuse University.

10. John Humphrey Noyes, 1860s.
Courtesy Oneida Community Mansion House.

11. John H. Noyes and the Oneida Community, 1863.
Courtesy Arents Collection, Bird Library, Syracuse University.

12. John H. Noyes and Charlotte Noyes Miller,
North Tower of Mansion House, 1860s.
Courtesy Arents Collection, Bird Library, Syracuse University.

 CHAPTER THREE

Complex Husband

I have seen it stated that the true women
should be a combination of the maid, the
wife and the harlot . . . [those] characteris-
tics are combined in those three women. As
I look at it now, in a certain sense Abigail
Merwin represented to me the split bean
theory; Harriet A. Holton the theory of spe-
cial companionship; and Mrs. Cragin rep-
resented to me communism—the freedom
outside of split beans and marriage both.
　　　　　　　　　　—John H. Noyes,
"My Marriage With Harriet A., the Four
Principal Women in the Community,"
Home Talk (1867).

*T*he community was quick to offer Victor Hawley an al-
ternative lovemate to Mary Jones. "Mrs. Dunn asked
me to have a baby by Emma (Jones). I said Roswell and Alfred had cut Cornelius out I had rather not have one by her as
Emma & Cornelius expected to have one." Rather than perform in the service of the community and take up with his
lover's sister, Victor rejects the idea that he should do to Cornelius Hatch what his brothers have done to him. In short, he
rejects their plan, their control, and their morality. The
Jones-Hawley connection was certainly a close family one
since Emma Jones had had a child by Roswell Hawley in

1873. There is no hint in the diary that the notion of sleeping with his lover's sister or (in the world's terms) his brother's wife was at all a troubling idea.

The shock of losing Mary was powerful at first. There are indications, however, that Victor might submit to his fate and follow community rule and practice. "I told Mrs. Dunn today that I had thought of having one by Ida Loveland." Throughout this period his mind remains profoundly unsettled, and he turns to the diary to pen lovesick soliloquies: "I was sick at heart & never want a child & death would be better than living as I am, would that God had taken me home to rest." After rejecting a long list of possible mates and discovering that Ida Loveland is too young (nineteen) to participate in the experiment, his thoughts turn back to Mary.

As spring struggles to break through the long New York winter (there is a snowstorm on April 30), Hawley's diary speaks again and again of Mary. "Often my thoughts are on thee Mary wondering if you have got started this time"; "When shall I walk with you again. Oh that you were here or I were there if only for an hour Would to God that you were with me forever." Early in May he begins to record a new set of mundane daily routines as if in an effort to throw off the pain of separation; he records the number of hours he works each day and his use of the Turkish bath. His central preoccupation, however, forces itself back into the diary: "I had been thinking before I went to sleep when shall Mary & I have a child and praying to God that we might have one."

During this period Victor begins to experience sympathetic, almost couvadelike pains that he associates with Mary. "At work in the Job Office 6½ hours. A hard head ache afterwards & went to bed after dinner till meeting time. Perhaps Mary is unwell and the feeling came over me during meeting time that she was & that that was why I felt so." Increasingly, the diary is filled by the minutiae of daily life, though there are occasional lapses when his emotions break his reporting of the pedestrian rounds of his life. "I helped get in Aunt Jane Kinsleys bed for M. P. P. Then went to ride with Frederic to W. P then to the Castle up the Indian road to 5 chimneys then to Gordon Place & home. Tears came down my cheek on the way . . . . Shall I ever take a ride with thee again Mary" (May 7).

Earlier in the week he had been wakened from a dream by the words "8 years the 4th August"—presumably the first time he and Mary had sexual relations. Emerging from his subconscious, the date is a dramatic reminder of how long and deep his exclusive relationship with her has been. It has taken possession of him; yet there is no sanctioned outlet for such love. In order to put that "special love" out of his mind he throws himself into projects that help to numb his feelings. For example, after spending five or six hours at the printing office Hawley then devotes his evenings to fixing items for other colony members, or working on his insect collection. Work will not drive thoughts of Mary away. "After meeting I had a crying time not a word do I hear from Mary." Feeling abandoned and unable to wait for word from her, Victor sends a short note asking "how is it this time," but there is no recorded answer. At an evening meeting Erastus Hamilton, a colony elder, makes the suggestion that "we all turn a Shaker for a while," and that suggestion offers little comfort to Victor, who feels that he is "one already & expect to be for years if Mary is started or perhaps forever. I might as well be a Shaker as to live here as I do."

The tensions and problems within the society in May 1876 were at an all-time high, with the elder Noyes's resignation and resentment growing daily over Theodore's leadership. In addition to the succession question there was the debate over stirpiculture that centered on the explosive conflict between community and individual needs. All this is mirrored in Victor Hawley's diary. While others are participating in the rich social life of the colony he spends his free moments walking in the woods, ruminating about his fate, and wondering just how long the separation will last; "a lonesome and sorrowful day no one cares to walk with me for Mary is gone." Finally, a note does arrive from her saying that she feels the "separation heavily." Quickly, he puts together a parcel and sends it to her via another member, despite his anxiety that it might be opened or intercepted.

As buoyed as Victor is by her note, it opens a new vein of

anxiety in him. *"Waiting, Waiting,* oh how long will it be,"* he writes on May 26. He fears she has abandoned him and taken a new lover. "Now that my friends think that my trials are past they say little to me, is it to be so with you Mary & will you forsake me too." His acute distress is exacerbated by a toothache that sends him first to the Turkish bath and then to bed. His emotional pain has become so severe that he is now unable to sleep with the young children in the community because they remind him of his loss. To add further to his woes, Victor learns on May 31 (from Theodore Noyes) that he is to cut off all contact with Mary. "Mary and I must not correspond & Mrs. Dunn made me promise not to."

The order to break off written communication has the opposite effect than the one intended by the leadership; Victor resolves to go to Wallingford to see her. His determination to do so is supported by a letter from his father saying that "Mary wants to go," confirming his own feeling that now is the time to break with Oneida. On June 2 he writes to John H. Noyes saying that he and Mary wish to go away. As if to further strengthen his resolve to pursue an independent course, Hawley writes to Mrs. Dunn, saying "that I did not wish to promise never to write to Mary." Despite this new-found determination, he remains in a state of emotional turmoil waiting for Mary to write to him and wondering, "why don't Mary write to me?" The days drag on for him. "A long & dreary day. I long to see thee but I may never.Oh God why is it when will the end be of this my *aching* aching heart had far better be torn from my body than wrung it is by slow torture."

While undergoing this emotional anguish Victor is still under constant pressure from the colony elders to commit himself to the community; they have not given up on him. Early in June James Towner gets a commitment from Victor that he will stay in the community and help "Mr Noyes and the community." After making the statement, he doubts his own ability to keep it, and, as if to mark this disbelief, his toothache flairs up again and his face swells.

After his tooth is pulled, Hawley enters a calm period; however, his dreams suddenly take on a profound meaning and recapitulate his anxieties vividly. His sense of abandonment is obvious. "I dreamed that the cars were going by and one was off the wheels & the rest of the train went on & left it . . . . I dreamed someone was skating on a river then there was an open water & a boat load of persons passed Mary was in it weeping with a thin and downcast face." Again Hawley tries to use work as an antidote to loneliness and anxiety as he busies himself with insect collecting, outings with the colony members, and again on one occasion the care of community children; yet, like the dreams, his thoughts return to Mary Jones, despite his best efforts to put her out of his mind. "I will try to read out the long hours that I am not at work but the tears will come even over the book. Burn on till life's torments are ended. None know the pain I endure but God may he end them soon."

Victor's diary has truly become the "hearer of my burdens" and becomes the one place where he can express his anguish. There is little formal religious sentiment in the diary, though he remains commited to the Perfectionist ideal. One sees in the diary rather a personal cry for understanding, a search for a sympathetic ear, since he has no friends to whom he can turn for intimate conversation. Sanction for his feelings comes from the diary.

During July and August Hawley intensifies his bird-collecting efforts, and his work in the printing office settles into an agreeable routine. Days roll by in an uneventful fashion, and Mary slowly drifts out of the diary, though she is not replaced by anyone else. Summer is monotonous. On Monday, July 31 Victor simply records that he has been "printing envelopes and cutting silk labels," and then on the following Wednesday all he can report is that, in addition to cutting more labels, he bent some "wires for a net for Mr. Warne" and took home some oak leaves for "Mrs Sears Polyphemous caterpillars." To others at Oneida Victor seemed to have accepted his fate and appeared "cheerful and happy" and was— in response to a query from Edwin Nash about his situation— trying "to make the best of it."

In late August Edwin Nash brought Hawley some words about Mary, and they were reassuring ones in that they paralleled Victor's own state of mind. Nash reported that she was "cheerful most of the time occasionally despondent but growing less so." It was Victor's first news of her since her departure in early April, and he inquires about where she sleeps and works. Time apparently has begun to heal the pain of separation for both of them. As if to confirm this tendency, he records that in early August he has obtained momentary relief from his aching tooth. The community dentist drills into a nerve cavity giving "relief for the nerve was dead." Seemingly, Victor's passion for Mary was likewise dead, if we are to gauge by the references to her in the next three months. Even though she was in Wallingford, news of her could not have been very far away. A letter was read, for example, on August 26 that must have stirred old memories. It is from Theodore Noyes (then at Wallingford) describing that there was someone there who had "a strong desire to have a baby (I knew he was speaking of Mary) & he thought of about twelve men who had not the strong desires she had but ought to be willing to put themselves in for public service." Hawley's diary entry for that evening indicates that his emotional attachment to her was far from dead and that it had been kept under control only by constant work.

What the diary reveals at this time is a man on the point of a breakdown, not someone involved in a grand experiment; a man torn by his devotion to a lost love rather than to any community ideal; a man living with a gnawing fear that he had lost her and their child to another man. "It was long past midnight when I went to sleep. It seemed as though a knife was going through me when the letter was redd. Of God shall we ever have a child? This has been a day of hard trial to me and I have had to fight hard to control my feeling. May God help me through it for it seems the hardest blow of all that she is able to have a baby by someone else. I could stand it well enough before but now it stings me through and through."

After this outbreak Victor's recorded life returns to its routine, with September and October repeating the pattern set in the earlier months of the summer: work, service to others, and an occasional lament about Mary's absence. Other couples who participated in the plan now begin to spend time together as couples while he and Mary are separated, "perhaps forever." The eugenics scheme obviously led to the formation of "exclusive" relationships and, in paradoxical fashion, the plan proved what Noyes had preached all along: namely, that the propagative character of sexual relations was destructive of community feeling and attachment. Maren Lockwood Carden, however, did note that those who wrote about community life were members of the elite central corps and that the dissatisfied left no record. The Hawley diary is not only the fullest diary we have, but it is one clearly critical of the experiment and of its goals and practices.

On November 2 Victor records his weariness. "I am tired tonight it has been a long wearying day & tears have come to my eyes many times and my heart aches but there is no one to care for me now." There had been no one to care for, or to care about since April; there is only routine, only emptiness, only the diary. The first Sunday in November brings startling news in the form of a letter from James Towner saying that "Mary would be here in a week or ten days." Hawley's ordeal is seemingly at an end, and one senses his belief that he has triumphed and fooled them all by working hard and "refraining from all connection with women."

A week later Mary arrives, and he exclaims, "O how my heart aches to be with her." His expectation that his sorrow will be turned to joy is dashed on Monday afternoon when— for the first time in eight months—he meets her. *"I met Mary* at 4.15 PM near the childrens room and shook hands & kissed her. at 5.45 went to her room where Mr Dunn has roomed. She told me what she has been through & that she had got started by Theodore the 22 of Sept. My God My God what has she been through as well as I. Will they tear the hearts out of both of us. when shall we ever be happy together."

The worst possible turn of events has taken place. Required to keep apart because of her unsanctified desire to have children, she is now pregnant by the leader of the colony, Theodore Noyes, the chief exponent of scientific mating. "My God My God, what has she been through as well as I." Victor Hawley has not only been thwarted but defeated and humiliated. His task is now, ironically enough, to become

Mary's servant, to care for her in a personal and loving way, to see her through a difficult pregnancy, to assume a surrogate role, and to help bring into the world the baby he wanted to father. Although instructed by the community elders to keep away from him, Mary seeks out Victor on November 15: "Fixing the alarm till 10 after meeting then went and saw Mary she had been looking for me. She went to bed in a few minutes and was cold. I got 3 hot flat irons & put in her bed I rubbed her feet and legs."

With Mary's return the second part of the diary comes to a natural conclusion.

The Diary of Victor Hawley
April 12, 1876–November 15, 1876

Wednesday April 12 1876
A dreary forenoon, out of doors till 11.30   F Marks came to my room I told him how I felt. I had a spasm about 12.30 & life seemed nearly ended for a few minutes. MDP brought my breakfast & dinner at 2 PM. Mrs Dunn asked me to have a baby by Emma   I said as Roswell & Alfred had cut Cornelius out I had rather not have one by her as Emma & Cornelius expected to have one.

Thursday April 13 1876
I told Mrs Dunn to day I had thou ght of having one by Ida Love land. F Marks had a list of names which he read off to see if any of them would suit me   I told him to keep on as none suited. I was sick at heart & never want a child & death would be better than living as I am, would that God had taken me home to rest.

Friday April 14 1876
I went to the Job Office & worked 1½ hour to day. Mrs. Dunn said Ida is 19 yrs & is to young   I said let it go then and about made up my mind to tell her I never wanted a baby but I thought I would get a note Mary said she left in the silk stockings in her trunk   I searched 2 hours for it & found it at 7.30 PM A thrill of peace and re-consiliation to my heart

which will make life easier for days and years to come I hope
for it has been a life & death struggle to me. Edwards Butterflies received

Saturday April 15,1876
I have worked 5 hours in the Job Office. I only slept 2 or 3
hours I went down and sat in the Nursery Kitchen from 12.30
till 3 to see if I could get sleepy. Life is dreary and I am weary
Oh God when will the end be ? My aching heart and burning
head have no rest. Oh God give me peace & happiness or take
me home to rest Gave Mr Angel my watch to clean

Sunday April 16,1876
Filing letters. Walked to Mud Creek with F Mar ks it
rained I had my overcoat & we had umbrellas The hours seem
longer than days & days longer than weeks or months as life
drags through them

Monday April 17, 1876
I went to the Job Office to work. My head ached allday
but I kept at it till 3.30 & made out 6 hours work

Tuesday April 18, 1876
5 h work at the Job Office My head ached so that I quit at
two oclock and went to see if Mr Burnham would give me a
bath but he was gone so I came to the house and took one.
Martha boiled some meat for my dinner. Oh how the blood
rushes to my head it seems at times as though the arteries
would burst.

Wednesday April 19, 1976
Hard head ache even harder after a T. bath at the Arcade
which was my first there. Fathers note to Alfred says that
Mary asked Ann why they did not let us have a baby. Ann
said on account of stirpiculteral principles Mary said if she
had known that she would have given it up long ago. *I said
how can that be* for they asked me to have one by Emma who
is not as well as Mary & Herbert was a weakly baby till Mary
nursed him.

Thursday April 20, 1876

I went to Marthas room after breakfast with a hard head-ache, she had me lay down and she put hot cloths on my head. I had a hard spasm or fit with severe cramping of my arms & legs which were nearly bloodless Last night about 10.15 I heard a voice say *"Do you know that Mary Jones is dead"* so forcibly *that I awoke suddenly*

Friday April 21, 1876

My head ached so that I could not eat half of my breakfast amidst the noise of the dining room. A committee at 10 AM W H W. W A H. M J N. Alfred. F A M. H A N. J A K. Chloe M D P. L K D. I was told to clear myself from special love and the spirit I was under and look for something to be thankful for & for words of obediance. Abed till dinner time, after dinner wrote a note to the family. I can hardly walk. Martha brought me 3 oranges

Saturday April 22,1976

Some better. Martha brought up my breakfast before I got up. Bath at the Arcade at 9.30 in hot room 35 minutes a se-vere head ache for more than an hour after the bath I sat in the summer house when I started for the house I saw a male and female red throated Woodpecker I shot them for Cor-nelius with his pocket gun.

Sunday April 23, 1876

I went to the dining room to my meals. I had some currant drink for dinner yesterday & last night & my meals last me more than 2 or 3 hours Turkish Bath at 9.45 in Hot room 15 minutes. I went to bed when I came back at 11.30 til 1.30 I went down sentimental walk & found a chrysalis. In Mrs Sears room after dinner she had a {female sign} Luna moth. I got some carbolic acid to kill red spiders on my vines [SH] tower

Mon April 24 1876

I went to the swamp before breakfast & took Cornelius pocket gun but did not get any birds Turkish Bath 9.45 in hot room 15 minutes I went to walk after dinner with M D P Telegram for W H W & L K D to go to W C for consultation In meeting the thought came perhaps they will have me try with Mary if she does not get started with L B Leonrad this month.

Tuesday April 25 1876

Turkish Bath at 10.15 in the hot room ½ hour. Worked in the Job Office 4 hours I laid down on M D P's bed before going to dinner to get rested Hope is gone & life is sorrowful the rest of the day. Mrs Sears had two Luna moths hatch out today a Male & female.

Wednesday April 26 1876

Turkish Bath at 10.15 in the hot room 25 minutes Job Office 2 hours I went to the mill and fixed a box for the Luna moths for Mrs Sears and put three live moths in it. Played backgammon after meeting with Emma & Clarence

Thursday April 27 1876

T Bath at 10.30 in hot room 25 minutes not shampood for Mr Burnham is sick Worked in Job Office 4 h. I went to Bear Creek after dinner hardly any birds to be seen & I am lonesome & desolate Reports from W C to night & talk from J H N stops all propogation Many there are who blame me for it Oh God what shall I do ?

Friday April 28 1876

T Bath at 10.30 hot room 20 minutes Job O 5 h.

Mr Hamilton came this morning from W C to stay. Roswell gets up at about 6 A M and I get up soon after and am verifying my Coloeoptera to pass awasy the time & occupy my mind till breakfast and filing letters after dinner when I can be outdoors

Saturday April 29 1876

T Bath 10.45 in hot room 25 at 160° I have had to have low heat ° & 150° on account of tendency of the blood to rush to my head but can increase the heat some now. J.O. 5h. Milford went to Syracuse. I printed envelopes on the fastest speed from engione & press at 20 lbs pressure. Answered G D A's letter about a watch

Sunday April 30 1876

T.B. 10m hot r 18 m at 170° I went over to see the new barn walls before breakfast with Fredric Verifyin Coleopltera List from 11.30 till 3.30. Went to walk after dinner & came back in a snow storm. I wrote a letter to Father.

Monday May 1 1876

TB 10 m hot R. 23 at 178° JO 5 h. Printing Waste Silk Envelopes on fastest speed 40 lbs pressure At 6.30 PM I walked down the railroad to the cheese factory and got back in time for meeting. Often my thoughts are on thee Mary wondering if you have got started this time. Time is cut short for you this year as well as last year.

Tuesday May 2 1876

T.B. 10.50 in hot R. 27 m. at 180° going down to 170° J.O. 5½ h. I walked down to the middle of the swamp after meeting. When shall I walk with you again. Oh that you were here or I were there if only for an hour. Would to God that you were with me forever.

Wednesday May 3 1876

T.B. 10. in hot R. 27 m. 190° In my sleep last night these words came so forci bly that I awoke "8 years the 4th of August" I had been thinking before I went to sleep when shall Mary & I have a child and praying to God we might have one. Have we got to wait so long as that. Better late than never but the days are long. I walked to the Castle before meeting.

Thursday May 4 1876

No bath I have finished my course. At work in Job Office 6½ hours. A hard headache afterwards & went to bed after dinner till meeting time. Perhaps Mary is unwell the feeling came over me during meeting that she was & that that was why I felt so.

Friday May 5 1876

J.O. 3 h. Cleaning the N Tower I took out the double windows. I put some car bolic acid in my insect cases after dinner the parasites were at work in one case. The Seminary garret is a dingy cluttered up place for L. F. Dunn has been having a skylight put in for the Dentist Office. I am watchman I went to the Office to see the timetable N.Y.C.

Saturday May 6 1876

JO 5½ h. I was going to Oneida with Milford but the train was ahead of time 8 or 10 m. & I was not ready @ 2.38. After dinner I went up Bear Creek & shot two birds. Eilton Brooks came on the 5 oclock train.

Sunday May 7 1876

I helped get in Aunt Jane Kinsleys bed for M.D.P. the went to ride with Fredric to W.P. then to the Castle up the Indian road to 5 chimneys then to the Gordon place & home. Tear came down my cheeks on the way I felt so & F. slept for ½ hour on the Indian road shall I ever take a ride with thee again Mary.

Monday May 8 1876

Milford & I went to W.P. I put a sight Fredric's cane rifle which I gave him about 2 weeks or 3 ago for I did not know but I should shoot myself with it I felt so some of the time. Milford fixed some rules & sticks for the Socialist & some parlor skates.

Tuesday May 9 1876

Job O. 6 h. After dinner I went down and set up the names that I have been verifying of my Coleoptera I worked till meeting & after meeting till 2 oclock in the night & finished them.

Wednesday May 10 1876

J.O. 3½ h. At one P.M. Milford was at work getting the 2nd form of the Socialist ready for the press so he could not stop to give me a job and he said I could work on my list. I

arranged the names according to the numbers which took till
4.30 After meeting I had a crying time not a word do I hear
from Mary.

Thursday May 11 1876
J.O. 5¾ h. I sent a note to Mary this morning. Copy.
Dear Mary,
How is it this time. Not a word do I hear. The prospect is
that Martha is started.
I worked on my list after meeting till 11.30 at the Printing
Office.
My new watch has come $30.25

Friday May 12 1876
JO 7½ h. Printing Turkish Bath Bulletin & alphabet. Mr.
Hamilton proposed that all turn Shakers for a while. I am one
already & expect to be one for years if Mary is started or perhaps forever. I might as well be a Shaker as to live here as I
do. Oh my aching heart has no rest.

Saturday May 13 1876
6 h. J.O. Printing cards for Martin for the waiters room &
dining room. I worked in my insect list after dinner have got
the first & second proofs corrected.

Sunday May 14 1876
Fredric & Martha went over to the woods this forenoon for
a walk but I have had a lonesome and sorrow ful day no one
to walk with me for Mary is gone this separation how long is
it to last.

Monday May 15 1876
JO 6½ h Silk Bill for customers that buy silk why dont
Mary answer my note. I look for one every day

Tuesday May 16 1876
J.O. 6 h distributing
Finishing my list after dinner putting in comma's

Wednesday May 17 1876
J.O. 4¾ h A.S. 1¾h distributing.
A note from Mary this P.M. Milford brought it to the J.O.
to me. Milford was called up stairs and it was well for me that
he was for I could hardly hold the type to distribute I trem-
bled so. It showed that she feels the separation keenly. I wrote
an answer in the evening, sent it the 18

Thursday May 18 1876
J.O. 3 h. I had set of pherotypes taken this morning. Milford payed in printing. I copied my letter and went to put it in
Orrin trunk but it was not in his room during meeting left a
little package in his room but afterwards got it.

Friday May 19 1876
JO 6 h I put the package in Charlotte's trunk this morning before she & Orrin left for W.C. I wrote a note to Mr
Noyes but shall not send it till I get her answer.
I went down through the woods and shot 6 birds for Cornelius with Henry Hunter. They left at 7 A.M. & got to W.C.
10.30 P.M. Stopped at Utica for the fast train

Saturday May 20 1876
I went to Oneida with Milford on the 10.45 AM train &
back on the 12.20 I bought ½ lb. Brazil nuts & a glass of beer
after coming back we sat on the seat south of the fish pond for
an hour

Sunday May 21 1876
I helped Mr. Reve's put down a carpet in Jane Abbotts
room where Theodore used to room I took Allan down by the
cottage for two hours before dinner then went to Spring Grove
with Clarence during dinner After dinner got a Purple
Grackle's nest and blew the eggs.

Monday May 22 1876
JO 3½ I took a lesson of Cornelius at 1.30 in skining
birds, he skined 2 & I skined 4 the last one in ½ hour. Sunday
eve a talk was read which refered to a criticism which I

thought was to Mary. Oh what anxiety it gives me for perhaps they have opened my package.

Tuesday May 23 1876

JO 6 h. puting in a new type stand & moving one up stairs
& another down. I read over the journal and talk from W.C. &
find that the criticism was Friday before Orrin & Charlotte
Maria T got there so I am at rest about the package   I went
to the swamp and shot 7 birds for CCH before meeting

Wednesday May 24 1876

JO 4 AS ½ Henry Hunter & I went to the swamp & shot 9
birds for Cornelius before breakfast. At 9 AM I went to the
Dentist Office & had LF Dunn examine my teeth. A hard
head ache the latter part of the day but it is better to night

Thursday May 25 1876

JO 2½ h. L.F. Dunn filled 2 teeth with Amalgam & one
with Hill's Stopping which took from 10 till 12 oclock After
dinner I went to the head of the gulf & shot 2 Indigo birds 2
Thrushes and some other small birds. Milford is going trout-
ing tomorrow & I am strongly tempted to go to W.C. tonight
or shall I wait for her answer.

Friday May 26 1876

I filled part of my cartridges. Cornelius was going to help
skin the birds at one but the fast mail train run off the track
and was 3 hours late. I skinned 5 birds. *Waiting Waiting* oh
how long will it be. I got ½ Doz pairs of Marino stockings

Saturday May 27 1876

JO 5½ h. T. Bath at 3 oclock 180° in hot room 20 minutes
Finished loading my cart ridges this morning. After made
some lemonade for Milford & Manly who were mowing the
lawn then went over to see the new barn with Fredric. Now
that my friends think that my trials are past they say little to
me, is it to be so with you Mary & will you forsake me too. Oh
God I hope and pray that you will not.

Sunday May 28 1876
I worked at the mill most of the day making spaces my insect list Fredric was there part of the time at work on a toilet bureau.

Monday May 29 1876
JO 6½ h Milford & I took lunch at 12 & I did not come to dinner but put into my list the spaces & took 15 copies of the list before spaced & after, before I got through I had a hard toothache. I took a Turkish bath & Martha made a molases & ginger pollice during meeting, I went to bed and finely got to sleep but awoke before *1* oclock the tooth ache was gone but I did not sleep any more.

Tuesday May 30 1876
JO 6h A Socialist 2¾h after dinner. I took my pants to be mended this morning. Clarence & I played backgammon from 9.45 till 10.45 to night. He asked me to take his place tomorrow fore-noon taking care of the babies but I told him I did not want to

Wednesday May 31 1876
JO 6h Mrs Dunn came up at 7 this morning & asked me if I would sleep with Haden in Edwards place. I told her I had rather not at present. Little do they know how it makes my heart ache that I cannot have one by Mary tears came in spite of me. I like the boy but it would only be torture to me to sleep with him now. She came to the JO & read me a letter from Mrs L. in which Mr. Noyes said Mary & I must not cor-respond & Mrs Dunn made me promise not to.

Thursday June 1 1876
JO 4¾h I got up at 1.30 and went to Oneida to see if I could go to Utica and get on to the 6.00 oclock train for Al-bany & W.C. but could not, got back 4.30. I told Fredric I wanted to go away with Mary. Two letters from Father to night Mary wants to go & I do with her.

Friday June 2 1876
JO 5h. I sent my letter to Mr. Noyes this morning that

Mary & I wanted to go away & a short note to Mrs Dunn saying that I did not wish to promise never to write to Mary. A letter from Mrs Skinner & a note from Mrs Dunn. I answered Mrs Skinner & wrote to Mary A T Bath with Fredric

Saturday June 3 1876
I distributed by insect list this morning . . . .
JO 5½h. Why don't Mary write to me. Persons ask me to take their babies & being asked to sleep with Haden since I have lost all hope of having one by Mary makes life but a torment I went to Oneida to get my watch fixed as it sliped off the bed & has stopped 2 or three times

Sunday June 4 1876
A long & dreary day I long to see thee but I may never. Oh God why is it when will the end be of this torment my *aching aching heart* had far better be torn from my body than wrung as it is by slow torture. My God help me

Monday June 5 1876
I told Fredric I should probably stay in the[SH] community. I went to Oneida with Milford. After dinner Mr Towner asked me to go to his room, he read a letter from Mary. I promised to stay in the community and that I would do what I could to help Mr Noyes and the community

Tuesday June 6 1876
JO 6¾h It seems hard to keep my promise but God help me I will do the best I can. I copied a letter that I wrote to Mrs Skinner last night and sent it this morning

Wednesday June 7 1876
JO 6h Tooth ache a Turkish Bath & a poultice on my face when I went to bed.

Thursday June 8 1876
JO 6h The pain in my face has left the right side & gone into the left side My face is swolen & I asked Mr Dunn to pull a tooth that aches the hardest he said I had better stand it till morning & then it be better.

Friday June 9 1876
JO 1h But little sleep I went down into the Nursery Kitchen at 2.40 A.M I could not work my face ached so I asked L.F. Dunn to pull a tooth this morning he said he would have to pull 3 or 4 or more I would not let him. I asked G.E.C. if it was neuraglia he said no my face would not swell so if it was

Saturday June 10 1876
Phebe made a ginger & C. peper & alcohol poultice & put on to my face last night   I went to bed but got up at 11.30 & went down to the N Kitchen for the rest of the night. I slept about 3 hours midst the pain and torture a hot freestone eases it a little with the poultice, but my face is badly swollen-
Martha rubbed it with alcohol and put on another poultice to night

Sunday June 11 1876
My face feels better & the swelling is going down. It has been 3 days & nights of torture A dull ache but very severe my food is mostly porrige for I cannot chew anything or hardly get my teeth apart.

Monday June 12 1876
JO 5½h Fixing coal bin My face is getting better

Tuesday June 13 1876
JO 6h Distributing A change has come I feel humble but not so down hearted or dis couraged. Thank God for giving me rest and peace from the torment

Wednesday June 14 1876
JO 5h AS 3h I sent a letter to Geo Dimmock with Coleoptera list & $1.00[SH] for Lables

Thursday June 15 1876
JO 6h I weigh 124 lbs I sent a letter to Mrs Skinner
Reading Frank Leslie's Monthly after dinner on the lawn.
I dreamed that the cars were going by and one was off from the wheels & the rest of the train went on & left it.

Friday June 16 1876

JO 1h I went to O Brien's Managarie & Circus at Oneida this after noon. Mary is not here to go with me Well do I remember our going to see the baloon Shall I ever see you again or take another ride with you.

Saturday June 17 1876

JO 5h I dreamed someone was skating on a river then there was open water & a boat load of persons passed Mary was in it weeping with a thin & downcast face. I layed down about 6 this evening and went to sleep and was waked up by Leonora laughing at the foot of the tower at 9.20 PM.

Sunday June 18 1876

I did not go to sleep till after 12 last night I was out walking the Flower Garden alone and in the arbor near the Dunn Cottage till 11 with an aching heart. This day has been long and dreary. Oh when will this warefare end. Would that life's sorrows were past or that life were ended. I took a gilt case from Mr. Warne's room to the Seminary garret. Parasites in 3 cases.

Monday June 19 1876

JO 6h I shewed Mr Hamilton a copy of my note to Mrs Skinner dated June 15   He had some talk with me & read a few verses from the Testament. I will try to keep in the true faith. I went to Oneida & got another glass for Mr. Warnes Insect case

Tuesday June 20 1876

JO 6h My heart still aches for thee Mary.

After dinner I got a thermometer from the Dye house & put into the Kitchen oven and I put in 12 cases of insects and heated them up to 180° for ½ hour to kill the parasites 8 worms were found dead from the baking

Wednesday June 21 1876

JO 5h AS 3h After meeting I helped Chloe & HMW put up our dinner for tomor row then I took a bath and got ready which took till 11 oclock

Thursday June 22 1876
I got up at 4.35 to get breakfast & Chloe, Harriet, Mr Warne & I started for Chitenango falls at 6.52 we had a fine ride & got there at 12.15 and took our dinner at the top of the falls then went below and had a long look at the falls the water was high from the late rains & it was a fine sight. Start home at 3. via Canastota got home at 8.35. will Mary ever go there with me.

Friday June 23 1876
JO 6h I put 14 cases of insects into the oven & heated them up to 200° for ½ hour after dinner and I had to go to the Seminary and hang them up after meeting I put in camphor and carbolic acid to keep out the parasites. Milford left for the lake in 3 P.M. train

Saturday June 24 1876
JO 6h Printing Fruit Dept. Pay Envelopes & a notice to visitors for Mr Easton Reading Frank Leslie Monthly after dinner

Sunday June 25 1876
Papering an insect case for Mr Warne Mary Prindle asked me to go to ride after we went with Elliot to WP then to the Castle up to Goake's place then west to the Indian road & then to the castle & home Via Hubbards.
Elliot drove about 4 miles

Monday June 26 1876
JO 2½h At work with Mr Warne arranging a case of Insects for the school room. We got the Insects in by 11. & I worked till 12.30 then went to the Job Office. After we hung up the case in the school room & carried Mrs Sears boxes of Insects to her room & hung up mine in the dark room. It was a busy day

Tuesday June 27 1876
JO 5¾h Printing Trap Circulars

Wednesday June 28 1876
JO 3h A Socialist 3½h Oh how my heart aches I will try to read out the long hours that I am not at work but the tears will come even over the book. Burn on till life's torments are ended. None know the pain I endure but God, may he end them soon.

Thursday June 29 1876
JO 6½ hours cutting paper for Fruit Labs & printing the first impression on Cherry Lables

Saturday July 1 1876
8 hours Job Office connecting the engine pipe with the engine which used to be in the Dentist Office & we are going to try to run the Job Presses with it.

Sunday July 2 1876
Reading Frank Leslie's Monthly I commenced the March No. last Friday evening and finished it this evening.

Monday July 3 1876
7 hours putting in pipe to engine & have got it running

Tuesday July 4 1876
I slept in Emma's place in the first bed room in the East Room with Herbert George W & Joanna. I made a bach of ice cream. A Teanant house burnt at the foundry I went over after going to the office to telegraph, then to the top of the tower & to the alarm room. I help ed carry water to save the old store house by the side of the pond

Wednesday July 5 1876
Job Office 6¼h printing slips for the Office.

Thursday July 6 1876
JO 5¾h at W.P. most of the time making a bush for a pulley to go on to the small Dental Engine

Friday July 7 1876
Job Office 6½ hours printing bronze labels for Silk Dept. I run the Gorden press from the small engine

Thursday July 13 1876
JO 6h cleaning the ink fountain and roolers of the Campbell Press so we can print Fruit Labels on it as the Uniersal Press is broken   Milford gone to Syracuse for ink &c.

Friday July 14 1876
JO 8½h I went to the Carpenters Shop and got some furnature for the Fruit Labels & we got the form made up so that I cammenced printing Labels of yellow at one oclock on the Campbell Press.

Saturday July 15 1876
JO 7½h Printing Frt. Labels I went to ride with Martha at 3 P.M. we took along some dinner for Fredric Marks Florence Clark & Ellen Nash. We had our dinner among some rocks on the West Hill. Martha & I rode back via Oneida Cemitary I had to drive slow on her account the others walked

Sunday July 16 1876
I got a Bluebirds nest which Mr New house thought was a Golden Woodpeckers nest it was in a tree near Mr. Hubbard's hop yard. I caught a few small butterflies & broke my net it is the first time I have used it this year.

Monday July 17 1876
JO 15½h At work printing Fruit Labs

Tuesday July 18 1876
JO 6h Finished printing the green on Fruit Labels Milford & I run the Campbell press last night till one oclock I went to the shop after dinner & mended my net.

Wednesday July 19 1876
JO 6½h American Socialist cleaning the ink fountain roolers &c

Thursday July 20 1876
JO 6¼

Friday July 21 1876
JO 7h

Saturday July 22 1876
JO 5h Printing the pamphlet Mutual Criticism. I left for Joppa on the 3 P.M. train with Mr Warne C Marks James Vail Philena Hamilton Cosette H & Mrs DeWolf we found Mr Inslie Mr Campbell & Mrs Baker down there.

Sunday July 23 1876
Mr Warne & I went to Oneida Creek on the beach after breakfast then through the woods to Black Creek keeping the North side of it back till ⅔ of the way back then through the hemlocks where there was a road. It was a hard & tiresome tramp through the tangled vines & bushes which were dripping wet.

Monday July 24 1876
Mr Warne & I went nealy to North Bay then south nearly a mile on the railroad then back through the woods to Joppa. It was better walking & not so wet. The mosquitoes tormented us some but not half as bad as they did yestuerday. I shot 12 Plover to day with my cane gun 2 of them were Killdeer.

Tuesday July 25 1876
James & Charles walked home yesterday early & Mrs DeWolf went on the cars. Mr Warne Cosette Ham ilton and I came home today I put 2 Attacus Cecropia caterpillars in Mrs Sears room with the other specime ns I got. I shot 3 Plover and a Robin.

Wednesday July 26 1876
JO 6h AS 1h My cane gun appears swelled inside of the barrel. Milford & I cracked some walnuts North of the Arcade after dinner then went & picked some black raspberries

Thursday July 27 1876
JO 6h setting Aspara gus Label & cutting paper

Friday July 28 1876
JO 7h printing Asparagus Labels &c.

Saturday July 29 1876
6h printing note heads & envelopes After dinner I went out with Milford & shot some Robbins he shot 3 & I shot 5

Sunday July 30 1876
I helped Mrs Sears fix the caterpillars in the boxes in her room in [SH]Hamilton Avenue. Finished reading last No. of Frank Leslie Monthly. I went to the Mr Hubbards with Henry Hunter   I caught a few butterflies & he shot a bird. I have commenced reading the Bible through

Monday July 31 1876
JO 6h Printing envelopes & cutting silk labels

Tuesday Aug 1 1876
JO 5h cutting silk labels

Wednesday Aug 2 1876
JO 6h Cutting Silk Labels
I went to the Machine Shop and bent some wires for a net for Mr. Warne and one for Rutherford after dinner & brought home some oak leaves from Mr. Hubbards woods for Mrs Sears Polyphemus caterpillars

Thursday Aug 3 1876
JO 6h Printing Bill Heads for Silk Dept. & the American Socialist 1½h.
At work on the net poles & ferules before breakfast & after dinner till meeting time at the Carpentars Shop

Friday Aug 4 1876

JO 6h Setting up a postal Card notice of a rise in the price of Raw Silk. Tooth ache nearly all day. I finished the net poles & varnished them. G.W. Hamilton said a man wanted us to take the Casinovia lock busi ness.

Saturday Aug 5 1876

JO 6h I dreamed that a large press was being moved into a room something like the Carpenters Shop where there was a lathe & I asked is the floor strong enough for the press. Mr Noyes has come and Edward Inslie has gone to W.C. to see Tirzah Miller but she & CA Cragin were sent to parts unknown

Sunday Aug 6 1876

I did not sleep but 3 hours last night. It was a bright moonlight night & my thoughts were far away at W.C. Edward is trying to see Tirzah. I went after oak leaves with FA Marks to Hubbards woods then down across the creek to the swamp & picked some blackberries after dinner.

Monday Aug 7 1876

JO 6h Destributing Milford went to Syracuse for Myron to see about a lithograph of one of our cows. Milford got me a knife

Tuesday Aug 8 1876

7h Printing Fruit Labels for bronzing

Wednesday Aug 9 1876

JO 5h AS 1h Printing Fruit Labs for bronzing for Jellies

Thursday Aug 10 1876

JO 3h cleaning ink fountain &c for printing Fruit Labels in red on the Campbell Press. I changed rooms with Clarence this forenoon as he wanted a light room to write out his meeting reports in. I room with Alfred in the South East corner of the Ton tine Garret. Good by to the N. Tower   I gave Holton a net frame & Augusta one

Friday Aug 11 1876

JO 6h I only slept 1½ hour it was so hot in the Tontine 83° when I went to bed I could hear 7 clocks toll out [SH] every hour of the night till 6 in the morning My heart is filled with prayer and yearnings for a child by Mary.

Saturday Aug 12 1876

An artist is giving Milford some instructions in painting.

I got some oak leaves for Mrs Sears then went to the W.P. shop fix my net frame.

Sunday Aug 13 1876

Henry Hunter & I mad two cans of ice cream for the family then went above the dam and went in swimming then I went off with Arthur Towner he for plants & I for butterflies I got quite a number & gave them to Mrs Sears.

Monday Aug 14 1876

JO 6h

Tuesday Aug 15 1876

12 h Printing red on Fruit Labels on the Campbell Press finished at 10.15 P.M.

Wednesday 16 1876

JO 9¼h Printing Asparagus Labels &c on the Gorden Press

Thursday Aug 17 1876

JO 8¼h Printing Currant Labels & Waste Silk Envelopes I dreamed a few nights ago that Mary came to me to get a check for her trunk she put her hand in mine but nothing was said because Mrs Story was behind her. Mary had a hat on and & dressed in black.

Friday Aug 18 1876

JO 11¾h Fixing windows 5h printing verses 3h. Printing M Criticism 3¾h I dreamed last night that I saw Chloe M.D. Pomeroy J Kinsley & some others & perhaps Mary on some cliffs below me near a river, soon after Chloe was going up some stairs I was near them & Mary said wait, soon after I was leading Ruddy to his mother, afterward I was near the top of some stairs then by a roaring river where many were carried down among cakes of ice GEC & I were trying to pull away some cakes that were nearly crushing a fine young woman she said dont kill me we said we will save you & George E lifted her in his arms and disappeared down the torrent. I previously saw a train & cars off the track going across a corner.

Saturday Aug 19 1876
I went to Durhamville with Milford & shot 2 Plover about a mile beyond. My heart aches so I almost cried in meeting tonight

Sunday Aug 20 1876
I fixed 3 Potassium bottles one for Mary Velzer. After dinner I went to Hubbards hop yard and got some catapill ars for Mrs Sears.
I feel as though I had rather Mary had stabed me through the heart than to have foresaken me so the Bradleys are going to leave

Monday Aug 21 1876
JO 14h Printing Mutual Criticism &c got through at 12.15 in the night

Tuesday Aug 22 1876
JO 5½ hours

Wednesday Aug 23 1876
After breakfast Chloe Jane Abbott Daniel Abbott & I went to Peterboro and saw Greene Smiths bird house & grounds then home Via Clockville taking our dinner in the woods. I had the tooth ache most of the way home. Watchman with a hard toothache

Thursday Aug 24 1876

JO 4h Printing slips for the Office & opening the box from Hartford Ct. which contained a part of the Universal Press. Edwin Nash asked me how I was getting along now said that I appeared cheerful & happy. I said I hoped the worst was past & that I was tring to make the best of it. He said Mary was cheerful most of the time occasionally des pondent but growing less so. I asked him where she slept & where she worked. It is the first I have known since she went there L.F.D. drilled into the nerve cavity which gave relief for the nerve was dead.

Friday Aug 25 1876

JO 6½h printing Bill Heads & Satements 1500 for Oneida & 1000 Office sheets

Saturday Aug 26 1876

5½h putting Universal press together &c. A letter was read in meeting from Theodore about some ones having a strong desire to have a baby (I knew he was speaking of Mary) & he thought of about 12 men who had not the strong desires she had but ought to be willing to put themselves in for public service.

Sunday Aug 27 1876

It was long past mid night when I went to sleep. It seemed as though a knife was going through me when the letter was read Oh God shall we ever have a child? This had been a day of hard trial to me & I have had to fight hard to controll my feeling May God help me through it for it seems the hardest blow of all that she is going to have a baby by someone else. I could stand it well enough before but now it stings me through and through.

Monday Aug 28 1876

J Office 4½h changing type cases Off to Joppa with Edwin ash Olive Ann Nash Isabelle B. Elinor & Altheia the train was 1 h late, we left about 4 oclock   Mr Whitney met us at Fish Creek & helped carry down the baskets

Tuesday Aug 29 1876
We took Mr Spencers boat and all went to the point beyond Lewis point & took our dinner of roast corn melons &c in
the woods Mr W. sailed part of the way in his little boat &
joined us at dinner. In rowing to & from Lewis point it took
an hour each way, the waves came into the boat some when
coming back

Wednesday Aug 30 1876
I shot 2 Plover with my cane this morning. We took a
short row up the river after break fast then came home on a
hop pickers train. Mr Whitney struck sail & went to Lake
Port with an East wind in the morning & came back at 6 PM
JO 4h

Thursday Aug 31 1876
JO 2h then waiting on the table as there are 5 car loads of
folk on a picknic from Fulton
Otman was with them

Friday Sept 1 1876
JO 5h distributing &c Ann Hobert has come from W.C.
Edward is going away he came on to Scanectady with her and
has gone back to N. York where Mr Towner is to meet him
and settle with him. F Wayland has got me the book The Insect World $2.43

Saturday Sept 2 1876
JO 6h Printing Note Heads for the Office & Silk Dept.
How often do I wish Mary had taken a differ ent course I
would not be suffering now as I am with an aching heart Oh
God how long is this to last.
The turmoil in regard to Edward only makes me feel
worse.

Sunday Sept 3 1876
Drying insects in the Kitchen oven which Mrs Sears has
pinned out this summer. After dinner Emma asked me to go
butternutting with Martha Alfred Fredric CEB MVB & Mrs

Velzer There were about 40 persons under one tree near Mr
Petres before we got through

Monday Sept 4 1876
JO 5h Printing notices for the farm & picnic's God help
me God help me. Oh how long have I got to endure this aching heart. I dreamed that my brothers killed someone & I
buried them in a snow drift

Tuesday Sept 5 1876
I went to Clinton with Mr Skinner Mrs De Wolf & Mrs
Pomeroy it was a cold windy ride but we stoped at the Coleges
& saw the Museum Library Hall & the large Telescope which
was in the Observatory. They were put up two more towers
for Telescopes

Wednesday Sept 6 1876
JO 14½h Printing Silk Price List got through at midnight
Milford & I had our dinner brought down to us

Thursday Sept 7 1876
JO 6h Printing Fruit Price List

Friday Sept 8 1876
Moving my telegraph instruments from the N. Tower to
my room in the South E. corner of the Tontine Garret. At 5
P.M. I went to W.P. with John Norton & helped clean the
Alarm Battery then came back & cleaned the battery on this
end. We got through at 9.20 P.M.

Saturday September 9 1876
Fixing zincs & making a box for my battery. After dinner
Edson help-ed me run a wire from his room in the Mansard to
my room Via. the South Tower. All connections made and battery set up at 10.30 P.M.

Sunday September 10 1876
I was called by Milford at midnight & went cooning up at
the head of the gulf we did not get any we got back about 4

oclock and went to bed. After breakfast extended my ground wire on the coil & find the cuircet good. Abed most of the day. Went butternutting after dinner with Clarence Lorenzo H.G.A. Bitia ML Prindle.

Monday September 11 1876
I went to W Place Machine Shop and finished my cane net holder [SH] Ann H[SH]

Tuesday September 12 1876
JO 1h 2h helping Mr Abbott fix a faucet to a marble wash bowl in the mens sink room Helped John Norton from 1 till 9 PM on the alarm wire & battery We brightened all of the connect ions. Found one ground wire rusted off & another was nearly off at the Villa. We put in a new ground wire & the alarm works well again.

Wednesday September 13 1876
J.O. 5h A. Socialist 1hr Fredric & Martha read together nearly every evening. John Norton & Minerva work in the Fruit Dept & are often seen together evenings but Mary & I are separated for years perhaps forever

Thursday September 14 1876
J.O. 1h Milford & I went to Rome to see a Job Printing Press We also saw a good bird dog & a man about some powder I commenced testing the Alarm evenings in John Nortons place

Friday September 15 1876
JO 8½h Printing 1000 Tags for Silk & Hdw Depts 1000 slips for F. Wayland for A.S. & destributing got through at 7.30 P.M.

Saturday & Sunday September 16 & 17, 1876
JO 4¾ h Distributing & printing Mutual Criticism 2h. At 1.30 I went to a corn roast with Clarence, Mabel & Mary Boles on the Island. We had corn, sweet potatoes bread & butter, cookies, grapes & sweet pickles. We got back at 4.30 for Mary

B. had to wash dishes. At 10.30 Milford Mr Peterson & I went to Mr Barney Harts & then with him after Coons on the west hill but did not get any We got home at 4.20 this morning & went to bed. Commenced practicing telegraphing with Henry Hunter at 4 P.M. & DE Smith from 7. till 8 P.M. A rainy day.

Monday September 18 1876
JO 8h Printing Fruit Price Lists.
Henry Hunter is going to practice from 7. till 7.45 A.M.

Tuesday September 19 1876
JO 9h Printing Mutual Criticism &c.
Finished it today. Finished Fruit Price Lists
After dinner took a type cabinet to the mill to be cased & sent to N.Y. & exchanged for another.

Wednesday September 20 1876
JO 9h Printing Cards for Silk Agent. Tomatoe Labels for J.C. Ackley & setting up type for a small Silk Tag. After dinner empty ing cases of the old open type cabinet. Milford & I work till meeting time.

Thursday September 21 1876
JO 6h printing small Tags for Silk Dept.

Friday September 22 1876
JO 6h printing Silk Tags. I got up at 3.15 A.M. & went to the Deapot after Father & Mrs Mallory but they did not come but their trunks came Alfred was with me. Father & Mrs Mallory got here about 10.30 A.M. & Father came down to see me at the press room about 1.30 P.M.

Saturday September 23 1876
JO 6½h Finished Printing Silk Tags. I printed 1000 in 43 minutes or 48 minutes including all stopages and laying out on the press & table &c.

Sunday September 24 1876
I cut some card patches for my cane gun. Helped John

Norton clean the telegraph battery in the Office cellar. After dinner helped clear the Hall for a dance at 6.45 I danced with Maria Barron, Mrs Whitfield, Chloe, & Waltzed with Annie Kelly, & the Spanish dance with Emma Finished waiting on three tables

Monday September 25 1876
JO 8h Printing Peach Labels for cans. I was tired when I got through I eat my dinner in the cellar then lay down on my bed till meeting time instead of going to the paring bee

Tuesday September 26 1876
JO 8h Setting type fro the A. Socialist Advertising Page.

Wednesday September 27 1876
JO 11h Setting numbers for Silk Sample Cards & Printing Fruit Labels I was asked to sleep in Mrs Campbells Room so as to look out for MD Pomeroy who has choking turns I was tired & declined. Fredric M. slept there.

Thursday September 28 1876
JO 9h Putting a counting machine on the Gorden Press &c.

Friday September 29 1876
JO 6h Finished putting on the counting machine on the Gorden Press then printing covers to Mutual Criticism Books. I slept on a trundle bed in MD Pomeroys Room last night. I shot 3 Robins this evening.

Saturday September 30 1876
JO 8h Printing slips for F.W. Smith & Envelopes Milford took the Dentist Office boiler to the Mill to be boxed & sent to W.C.
Our New Type Cabinet came a day or two ago

Sunday October 1 1876
At work at the mill fixing a took for driv ing off caps from my cartridges & making a small board for loading. I slept in M D Pomeroy's room

Monday October 2 1876
JO 6h Fastening some Type cases together to send off. Putting on handles on to Type cases I have a boil on my right hand which makes it painful to do such work but I kept at it.

The boiler has gone Dr Carpentar took a fungus growth out of M.D. Pomeroys nose.

Tuesday October 3 1876
JO 7h Finished putting on the Type case handles & printing covers to Mutual Criticism. I slept in M D P. Room last night. she awoke quite often & called for drink. Milford is with his cousin yesterday & to day

Wednesday October 4 1876
7h JO Finished printing M Criticism covers then printed some sam ple sheets of type for sale   Milford has sold the Buergeois type. At 3 P. M. I took the small Engine to W.P. to have a new bolt put into the cylinder head & to have it put in good running order.

Thursday October 5 1876
JO 7h Printing Letter Heads & Note Heads for the Silk Dept.

I slept in MD Pomeroys Room last night

Friday October 6 1876
JO 4h Putting type into the new Cabinet.

At one oclock came up & helped Martha clean a room in the Lower Sitting Room as she is moving into the 1st West Room going from the Hall. Milford & I went to Durhamville to see light hand car

Saturday October 7 1876
JO 6h Milford & I went to Oneida to see hand cars on the 3 P.M. train & walked home in the evening. I slept in MDP's room.

Sunday October 8 1876
I went to the WP shop to look for wheels after breakfast, came home at 1.30 PM & Milford went over with me after look-

ing at the best wheels, we decided to make some. we went to the Carpenters Shop & sawed out some pine lumber for them

Monday October 9 1876
JO 4h we finished sawing out the circle of the wheels and bolted them together then sent them to W.P.
I slept in MDP's room.

Tuesday October 10 1876
JO 2h At work at WP on the Shafts for the Handcar & the wheels early & late before breakfast & after dinner till meeting time.

Wednesday October 11 1876
JO 1½h I slept in MDP Room I went to WP before breakfast to work on the handcar, came home to breakfast, went over with Geoff finished boring the wheels & turned them & sent them over, went to Smiths Oneida Dentist, saw Milford with the wheels. Decided to take them to Utica for tires. We waited till 9.30 P.M. for Mrs Hatch & Mrs Skinner they didn't come.

Thursday October 12 1876
JO 5h Milford has gone to Utica with the wheels.
Boring the crank wheel & making the crank shaft

Friday October 13 1876
JO 5h Frt. Labels. Making crank & pining on the wheel
Did not have to sleep in MDP Room as she is getting better

Saturday October 14 1876
JO 3h F Labels Finished the crank & making a handle at the Carpenters Shop.

Sunday October 15 1876
Milford Fredric Marks & I worked on the frame for the Hand car nearly all day. A dance at 5.45 Milford & I came from the Mill at 6 P.M. Chloe danced a Cortillion with which was all that I danced.

Thursday October 19 1876
JO 5h I came up at 2 PM & put up some provisions for Milford & I & we went to Joppa with John Cragin Elizabeth Kellogg Maria Barron & Maud EF Hutchens & Ransom

Friday October 20 1876
Milford & I got up at 5.30 went most to Lewis Point then to North Bay got a sail boat sailed down the North shore most to Frenchmans Islands then back to Cleveland where we stopped for the night getting there at 8 oclock Milford shot 3 ducks

Saturday October 21 1876
We started for home against a head wind ran across the lake in a rain storm stopped at Dr. Wilson's to get dry rowed the rest of the way to Lewis Point & N. Bay. A cup o tea then to Joppa getting there about 7.30

Sunday October 22 1876
Milford & I built a Bough House a the mouth of Fish Creek then after Breakfast we went to North Bay after my cane which I left there last night Maria B. & Arabelle went with us. C Marks Arabelle Mary Velzer, Otis, Mary Prindle & Elliot came in 2 carriages & left at 4. Mr Spencer & helper Milford & I went to L. Bay Mr S shot 1 duck

Monday October 23 1876
Milford shot another duck from the bough house & after breakfast Maria B. Milford & I came home. Mr Pitt, E.F. Hutchens stayed another day. Mr. P went down Saturday

Tuesday October 24 1876
JO 6h We hear that the centenial train which went by yesterday had a smash up one man killed. A number from this vecinity went but were not hurt.

Wednesday October 25 1876
JO 4h At 2 PM I went to W.P. & put on the rims to the car wheels   I got them on about 7.15

Thursday October 26 1876

JO 5h George Kellogg Milford & I made a break & put it on then got a team & took the car over to the deapot & tried we could hardly make it go on a down grade the belt wheel on the driving shaft was so small 6½" diam

Friday October 27 1876

JO 5h I went to the shop & got a 16" pulley, but afterwards got a better one from the Frt. Dept. & George & I put it on the car runs hard yet the face of the wheels are flat & when running crowd hard on the rims

Saturday October 28 1876

JO 5h The last two pages should be on Friday & Saturday. I was such a fine evening when George & I was at work on the car that we would have gone to Joppa if it had run easily.

Sunday October 29 1876

The track men are laying new rails across the trestle & I borrowed a new handcar & C Marks John Cragin James Vail & I went to Oneida & back in an hour GR Kellogg got on this side of the Castle when coming back

Monday October 30 1876

JO 6½h Milford & I went to Syracuse to get some paper & tools for the J Office & I got some rubber hooks then we tried to get some handcar wheels that were light but could not find any that were light enough. I stoped at Oneida to see a tel egraph line hand car but it had not come & I had to walk up.

Tuesday October 31 1876

JO 8h Fixing belt shifter to the Campbell press, broke off the head of the key trying to take off the flywheel.

E.H. Hamilton talked with Milford last night about the hand car feever that has got started among the young men

Wednesday November 1 1876

JO 9½h Printing Silk Price List & cards for G.D.A. We worked till meeting time.

Thursday November 2 1876
JO 10½h Printing Trap Circul ars. I am tirred to night it has been a long weary day & tears have come to my eyes many times & my heart aches but there is no one to care for me now.

Friday November 3 1876
JO 9¾h Puting a pulley on the line shaft and belt to the small engine so as to run the Universal Press from the small engine. Printing Trap Circulars

Saturday November 4 1876
JO 10½h Trap Circulars
I received a note this(crossed through)

Sunday November 5 1876
JO 8h Printing Trap Circu lars & Frt. Lab. I received the monograph of Geometrid Moths Presented by the author. *A note from* Mr Towner saying that Mary would be here in a week or ten days. Our building the hand car & my refrain ing from all connection with women makes them think I am going away. Packing M.D.P.'s things away in the garret 1½h I thanked him & said I hoped for the best results.

Monday November 6 1876
JO 6h Printing Frt Labels I helped MDP put away some more things in the garret before breakfast, after breakfast she asked me if I was getting along well or was tempted to go away   I told her I had some trials and temptations but was trying to hold still & make the best of it. She left for W.C. at noon with G.E.C.

Tuesday November 7 1876
JO 9½h

Wednesday November 8 1876
JO 10½h

Thursday November 9 1976
J O 8h

Friday November 10 1876
Milford & I went hunting squirrels, he shot 2 grey & one red one. I shot one red one. A lime team run into our buggy & tipped us over when coming home one wheel broken both tugs & the crossbar to the shafts broken. Goaks team

Saturday November 11 1876
JO 5h printing 6000 cherry labels bronzed.
George Ayers & I went after the broken waggon & he took it to Oneida Mrs Dunn said Mrs Skin ner wanted to see me I went to her room at 11.20 A.M. it was to find out how I felt in regard to Marys coming from W.C. I told her it would depend upon the position they wanted me to take towards her. Mary came at 7.00 P.M. I did not see her.

Sunday November 12 1876
I worked at the Sem inary on my beetles, I am going to send some Geo. Dimmock.
I have not seen Mary to day she came with Mr Towner & Lillian Oh how my heart aches to be with her

Monday November 13 1876
JO 6h *I met Mary* at 4.15 P.M. near the childrens room & shook hands & kissed her. at 5.45 went to her room where Mr Dunn has roomed. She told me what she had been through & that she had got started by Theodore the 22 of Sept. My God My God what has she been through as well as I. Will they tear the hearts out of both of us. when shall we ever be happy together again.

Tuesday November 14 1876
JO 4½h Cornelius stuffing a surf duck   I was with him in the Barn Office from 2.30 till 4.00 then I was in his room till meeting alone at work on beetles Cornelius shampooed Emma's head& they are together a good deal but Mary & I have to keep separ ate

Wednesday November 15 1876

JO 8h Fixing the alarm till 10 after meeting then went and saw Mary she had been looking for me. She went to bed in a few minutes & was cold I got 3 hot flat irons & put in her bed & I rubbed her feet & legs.

Thursday November 16,1876

J O I went to Stone's Woods after dinner with Milford he shot a re squirrel I did not shoot any

 CHAPTER FOUR

Special Love

We labor to perfect the individual but what we want is the art of multiplying copies of our work. Education is the waiting for the printing press and its printing press is to be scientific propagation.
— John H. Noyes,
Essay on Scientific Propagation (1875)

$\mathcal{A}$fter a period of prolonged separation Mary and Victor were reunited, and they began to grow closer as the child matured in her womb. Her second pregnancy was no easier than her first because during the first few months she suffered almost continuously from morning sickness. Victor's notations in his diary for the third week in November have a recurrent theme: "With Mary after dinner I got her some grapes which she liked very much and kept down she throws up everything she is so sick to her stomach; Mary is some better today but keeps to her room." Victor's attentiveness and concern about her condition is seemingly never compromised by his awareness that the child she is carrying is not his. Years of living in a community that emphasized mutual caring and collective child responsibility have left their mark on him. But his concern for Mary Jones is intensified, and for the community leaders it eventually becomes too intensive.

Oneida was a close-knit family in which the ideology of mutual aid was put into actual practice. For example, Victor aids in the delivery of a child by his sister Martha. Frederic, (the father), Mrs. Dunn, Mrs. Loveland (both older women), Emma Jo, and George E. Craigin (the physician) were all in attendance. It was a child sanctioned by the stirpiculture committee, and Victor must have watched its birth with particularly mixed emotions, though he records the event matter-of-factly.

At the same time Mary is in correspondence with Edwin Nash.

> Dear Brother,
> I fear you think by this time that I have forgotten you or that I do not intend to answer your notes, if so please don't think so any longer. I am real thankful to get your notes and I did mean to write to you long before this but I must say that the past four weeks have been about the hardest four that I ever spent. Until this week I have not been able to keep much of anything down some days I could not get up out of my chair without its making me sick to my stomach. I think I felt as Aunt Susan did when she had thrown up everything but her stockings but I am past that now and I am getting real smart! I go to walk every day I don't stop for wind or snow, I have been as far as the Hamilton Bridge today but the wind was blowing so hard and it was so stormy that Mr.Seymour went with me. Victor said that he hoped I would not go far alone for he was afraid I would blow away. I told him if he saw a water spoof flying through the air he might know that I was inside of it. My dear brother I should like to take a sleigh ride with you.
> Please remember you are not to show my notes.
> Your loving sister,
> Mary

Rather than being "hysterical," as she was later described, Mary Jones seems remarkably level-headed and good-tempered but in need of considerable attention during a difficult pregnancy.

During the next several weeks Victor is in constant attendance upon her, and they console one another. On December 16 she asks him if he were "tempted to go away" and he re-

plies, "I would give $50 if we were well out of this." Then, he
reports in his diary that they both "had a crying time, but she
is with child by T.R.N." Victor feels trapped by the situation
and is bound to Oneida now only by his love for her. If he
remains, his life will be bleak because, as his father reminds
him on December 19, he can "never have a child by Mary."

Realizing his acute sense of despair and loneliness, she
asks him to "stay with others," but he "cannot" and turns to
his diary to unburden himself. His despairing entry of December 21—the first day of winter—comes on a day when sun-
light was short.

As the days lengthened and the temperature dropped,
Victor and Mary come closer together despite the community
warnings. The last nine months have, he confesses, been full
of "sorrow & tears, with torture and pain, and aching heart
that no one knows of & tears would not ease." At this juncture
his pain and anguish is acute because the community has
placed her out of reach; yet she is within his sight and care
every day. The community has both created the child she is
carrying and prevented true love from taking its legitimate
course. They begin to spend every evening with each other as
he makes her tea and massages her, and, once again, they
make love. "I slept with Mary last night as she did not feel
well & I had to wake her every few minutes as she had slept
hard & was quite feverish till we had connection at 5am after
which she slept better." Early in January he writes, "Slept
with Mary no connection we cuddled down and slept as of
old." During the winter months they settle into a domestic
routine, with Victor caring for her; Mary often stays in bed
because she is unable to hold down food and is in a weakened
condition. "Mary is quite nervous & has the headache. She
was not dressed yestuerday or today but has to keep to her
bed most of the time. I sent for some oranges & . . . she has
eaten them after her meals to keep from vomiting." Victor's
own psychological state is equally uncertain, in part because
he has been shifted back to work in the dental office. Mary
and Victor see each other daily because he reads to her for an
hour from the New Testament. Though he confides to his fa-

ther that he "felt happier than I was a spell ago," he still has great mood swings, and his emotional balance is precarious. For example, shortly after making the comment to his father he attends a community discussion of stirpiculture that brings him to tears.

Conditions within Oneida remain tense during this period, with conflict over the operation of the stirpiculture plan; Theodore Noyes's leadership leads Victor's father, Julius Hawley, to say that because there was "so much turmoil in the Community that he did not want his children to have any [children] now." Victor had been denied his chance and secretly harbors a resentment against his father. "Little does he know how I feel at not having one by Mary. He has made my life bitter & I am far from happy." The elder Hawley was a staunch community defender and Noyes supporter, who took the colony's side whenever a dispute arose over his son's actions.

Occasionally, Victor has arguments with Mary; however, he remains remarkably attentive and sympathetic to her. For example, he cooks oysters for her since they are among the few foods that she is able to keep down. Their desperate need for one another comes through frequently in the diary. His entry for January 17 shows just how much they have come to rely on each other. "Mary came up to see me just as I was getting up. She said that she did not sleep any before twelve O'clock because I left her so. After dinner we had a crying time & I could not read the Testament without crying. . . . I left her & went down to the Nursery kitchen and saw Mrs Hall & then went back at 12:30 and stayed till 2 this morning. Sweet was the time."

"Sweet was the time"! After long periods of forced separation, Victor and Mary can find time to cry, to make love, to lounge with each other. They are now tranquil in each other's presence, eager to comfort and to be comforted. Mary's pregnancy remains difficult since she is continually stiff and sore. "I am going to rub her hips & legs as they ache they did not stop aching so I went to bed with her & had connection and all the pain left her." Days of sweetness and pleasure seem to be followed by days of despair, days when he cries and laments that he will never be happy. "Shall I ever be happy here. O why this turmoil of life it would be happiness if I could have a baby by Mary but now it is misery or hope long deferred, but I pray God to help me."

Mary is not only close to Victor but remains on intimate terms with Henry J. Seymour, the father of her first unborn child and someone considerably older than she. He was fifty-one. Seymour had been in the community since 1848, having been converted to Perfectionism by George Cragin. Helen Campbell Noyes, the wife of J. H. Noyes's brother George, was the mother of Seymour's first child, in 1850, and his wife, Tryphena (whom he married in 1847), bore his second. Mary Jones had a stillborn child by him in 1872. Seymour was the community horticulturist, and it was to him that Mary turned for help in 1877. References appear in the Hawley diary to her seeking out Seymour's advice, to her sitting in his lap during sick periods, and to his staying in her room. It is impossible to know whether she had sexual relations with him during this period; her remarks to him (reported in her letters) are centered on the weakness that some men show towards their own children—a charge usually levelled at colony women. Seymour, however, thought she was "thinking evil" and "he did not stay with her as he spoke of doing. She feels bad that he should do so."

Such critical remarks about attitudes toward the children reflected a growing split in the society over them. Children were no longer considered "community children" because there were a growing number of "exclusive attachments," represented by the Hawley-Jones affair, including Theodore Noyes's own relationship with Ann Hobart, who many thought exercised considerable influence over him. Charlotte Leonard reported on a "marriage ceremony" between Edward Inslee and Tirzah Miller that was part of an effort to keep Inslee in the community —"fastening him"— by having a baby with her. They kneeled together on the stage of the auditorium just after a small group had been ceremonially admitted into the community with the singing of the "Complex

Marriage Hymn." Miller and Inslee's song—to the tune of "Old Hundred"—was a "Blessing on Begetting":

> Our Father ! on these two who kneel,
> Our blessing with Thy blessing seal;
> And grant in coming joyous days
> A noble child may lisp thy praise.

The festivities were rounded off with Tirzah and Edward playing a duet; he on horn, she on piano. They eventually had a child, called Haydn; his name was changed to Paul by John H. Noyes when Edward Inslee left in 1875 in a bitter row.

During the long period when male continence had the support of everyone at Oneida there were only a few accidental births, and those children were easily absorbed within the "family." That practice could no longer be said to be true of the community in the late 1870s when sexual relations took place for the avowed purpose of having children. For, despite the altruistic rhetoric of the stirpiculture plan, it created individualistic tendencies rather than community-oriented ones. Clearly, such rhetoric had force and meaning for an older generation brought up in the Perfectionist and Bible Communism tradition and for some of the scientifically oriented younger group. These factors, coupled with the weight of Noyes's authority, his charismatic qualities, and the dominant position the elders had in the society, gave the stirpiculture experiment a powerful impetus. During the 1870s, however, that authority was questioned increasingly, particularly because it concerned an "experiment" that unleashed human passions and sexual needs in ways that had been kept in check and submerged for over twenty years.

The community, represented by Noyes, his son, and the elders, could still command a mature woman like Mary Jones (who wanted to have a child) to become pregnant by a man she did not love, or care for. What Victor Hawley's diary reveals is that such unions produced both alienation from community life and exclusive love affairs and engendered feelings of "philoprogenitiveness" in both men and women. This shifting from community love to private love took place, ironically

enough, within the context of an experiment that was intended to insure that Oneida would continue as a community
and that it would produce a perfect race and serve as a beacon
to the world. The experiment had the very opposite effect.

As Mary's child developed Victor began to record its
growth in her womb. By the end of January she is a little over
four months pregnant and measures 35½ inches at the waist.
During February he takes a different reading of her condition
when he places his hand on her stomach while she sleeps and
"felt the baby move 3 or four times" and the "night before I
felt it 10 or 12 times before I went to sleep." The worst of her
illness is past; he now replaces her as the sick one, coming
down with a severe cold. She now acts the part of nurse,
bringing him hot lemonade to help him sweat out the cold.
Other members of the community begin to note that they are
spending a great deal of time together. "Emma spoke to me
about Mary and I being together so much that it was causing
some talk. I told her that I would try & not disturb folks."

During January and February their life together is re-
laxed, despite the colony talk and comment. Hawley's diary
account of their life now focuses on two areas: their private
thoughts and the details of their life within two small rooms.
It is as if their world has been reduced to their own bodies, to
the activities that touch directly on their own space. One February weekend produces the following diary entry that illus-
trates just that sense.

> Changed Mary's bedstead so that she can get into bed
> easier. I slept with Mary last night . . . . . I swept Mary's
> room she does not feel well today as she did not sleep but
> little for two nights. Mr Seymour slept with her last night. I
> watched Mr.Higgins the last half of the night & he died at
> about 8:15 Mary did not get up till 11:30 a.m. About 1p.m. I
> went down and cooked her some tenderloin etc.

Cooking, sleeping, and ministering to the dying all domi-
nate Victor's life at this point. When Mary is five months into
the pregnancy, he notices the baby moving so quickly that he
can observe those movements despite a heavy layer of blankets on the bed. Though her morning sickness has abated,

Mary now suffers from insomnia and moves to a different room to get sleep. From late February to mid-March she is often weak and does not participate in community events. She and Victor continue to read from the Bible and, on occasion, attend dances. Whether their Bible-reading sessions simply serve as a justification for them to be together or Victor and Mary are earnest in their religious practice is difficult to gauge. They are focused on the birth of the child, and in mid-March an incident occurs that threatens the birth: a young child runs into Mary and pushes against her bowels with some force.

On the day after the incident Victor records that Mary is feeling better, and he expresses the hope that "her baby has not been hurt by Herbert." By late March Mary gives up waiting on tables and makes a telling remark to Victor: "Mary has had to quit work in the waiters room as she feels as though she had given away so much of her life to the children that she needs a rest." She needs a rest from community children in order to take care of her own body, her own child. This shift from community labor to personal care is emblematic of her own shift in priorities and consciousness. Subsequently, she was criticized by both her father and sister for her selfish attitude toward her work. "Emma talked so to Mary about her working that she had a crying time, and has thrown up her supper." At this time Mary is in correspondence with Seymour Nash, who is at Wallingford.

> My dear brother,
> Thank you for your many many kind notes I am always glad to get them and did mean to write to you oftener, every day I would think that I would write the next day but something would come up and take my attention or I would be to lazy to make an attempt. I presume that you have heard that I have troubled wit the Auge this spring it came to on soon after I got my little clothes done I consulted Doctor Carpenter the first of April he said needed toneing up and advised G.E.C to give me Port Wine Iron and quinine which I have taken ever since. I don't try any public work now.The doctor told me not to do anything to tire me, he said without a doubt the Auge was what weakend the other child so that

it could not be born alive. Dear brother you ask when my
time will be up if I go my full time it will be up the four-
teenth of June, but Carrie A. says she shall expect it any
day after the first of June. If you can come the last of the
month I hope you will for I shall be glad to see you before I
am sick. Don't show or read this to anyone. Alice sends love.
  Your sister for true courage.
  Mary
  Don't show or read this to anyone

That notation, "Don't show or read this to anyone," can be
found in the margins of many letters sent by members to close
friends. Obviously, there was a private world at Oneida distinct from the community world. Whether that split had existed prior to the 1870s is unclear, since the editions of Oneida
letters published so far fail to indicate such notations, but the
Nash papers reveal a significant number of them where there
are references to the need to maintain secrecy.

Now in her sixth month of pregnancy, Mary still has difficulty keeping food down, and she remains weak. Early in
April the community move to separate Victor and Mary. In
his diary he notes that Mr. Herrick "is to wait on her so I
must step out of the way." It is unclear just what Mr. Herrick
now does for Mary since Victor's diary continues to record
their Bible-reading sessions.

Other news comes at this point, and it is truly distressing.
Theodore Noyes, the father of the child, has arrived at Oneida
from Wallingford. Mary asks Victor "what made me so sober?" His answer, "It is Theodore's coming & thoughts of what
passed a year ago. I have to smother my feelings as much."
During the first half of April he sees little of her, and when he
approaches Mrs. Skinner about the possibility of Mary's coming to his room, he is told "no." "(Mrs Skinner) would not ask
her and said she was afraid my influence would be bad for
Mary & draw her down into a sickley state. They think the
separation is what helped Mary."

Clearly, Mary's sickly state had been brought on by more
than Victor's presence. Her complicated earlier pregnancy
and her anxieties about her separation from him both contributed to that state. From the community vantage point, how-

ever, Victor was someone who could "draw her down," cater to
her low instincts, bring her into "a state of disbelief," make
her his own rather than share her with the community. In
that sense he was a true threat because his influence took her
away from a proper ascending-descending social relationship.
Individuals were supposed to associate with those who would
"draw them up" by encouraging their spiritual state and min-
imizing their fleshly state; such individuals could coach
others along a path of spiritual perfection.

In many ways Mary's association with Theodore was a
model of that path. She was physically slight of body, and the
community might improve its "stock" by Theodore and Mary's
combining rather than by letting her have a child with a
lukewarm and physically unimpressive member such as Victor Hawley. She needed guidance, and there was no one better
equipped to guide her than the founder's son and now community leader. She was spiritually weak and he was presumed to
be strong, though many had come to doubt his spiritual
strength since it was rooted in a vague Comteanism rather
than in the powerful primitive Bible Communism of his father. Theodore could teach her something; he could be a
proper father for a child of the new race. That he was cold and
indifferent; that he had drifted away from his father's faith;
and that he cared little for Mary Jones made no difference.
His spiritual and social states were higher than hers, and
Mary could be "advanced" by his influence.

Louis Kern, in his *Ordered Love,* has argued persuasively
that Oneida was—from first to last—a society dedicated to
the propositions that women were inferior to men; that their
special "instincts" had to be controlled; and that in the "topi-
ary of Perfectionism" (his telling phrase) women were to be
pruned and held in restraint lest they grow wild and destroy
the symmetry of God's garden. "The need for control, for lim-
itation, for restriction of the sexual relationship, which was
central to Oneida's sexual ideology, suggests a certain sense
of guilt about the acknowledged pleasurable justification for
intercourse that Noyes considered paramount." In Kern's
view the male leaders at Oneida feared women as "predatory,
sexually aggressive beings, who vampire-like was capable of

draining men of their vital fluids, or worse still, of emasculat-
ing them, and leaving them spiritually, and sexually and so-
cially impotent" (228).

Noyes had denounced the selfish "I" spirit as early as 1846
and had consistently tried to limit the potency of selfish love
and to force it into a channel called "the community" that
would turn it into a social force that could revitalize society at
large. Sexuality was a powerful force and had to be held in
check, particularly in women. Men took full advantage of
their superior position within the community to pursue younger women before and during the stirpiculture experiment.
During the 1870s the younger colony women thought the new
scheme was a "mans game." According to Kern, "female discontent, then, was in part a persistent phenomenon, and ob-
durate adherence to the romantic love tradition . . . . The
maturation of the second generation of Oneida women and
the roughly coincident initiation of stirpiculture combined to
render discontent more serious and widespread in the 1870s"
(269). Male continence demanded self-control from the men,
and yet, the system still kept them in control of women
through the ascending-descending fellowship arrangement.
Such a scheme gave women considerable sexual freedom and
control over unwanted advances, but denied them true choice,
and when the opportunity came—during the stirpiculture experiment—it was the men who led and the men who controlled the system, primarily older men.

So Mary Jones's ultimate rebellion has to be seen in the
context of both her attachment to an older tradition of romantic love and her demand that she have, in the cliché-worn language of the 1970s, "control over her own body." Victor
Hawley was willing to give up his traditional (male) Oneida
prerogative in order to be loved and to love in a selfish way.
The symbol of that selfish love—that unsanctified love—was
a baby. It would be "their" baby, one conceived in sin, born in
sin, and raised in sin. Victor Hawley would not deny himself
Mary's love, her child, or her sexuality. He was bound to be at
odds with the society and its demand that he submit himself,
control himself, keep his love social rather than sexual and
individual. According to Kern, "It was this conflict between

the needs of the self and the ideals of the community that led to the breakup of the Oneida system of sexual adjustment and the reinstitution of monogamous marriage in 1879" (278). The Hawley-Jones affair prefigured that break-up.

Victor's separation from Mary causes him to lapse into an illness. She is able to return to her role as nurse and administers some "bitters of Balmany" (Oswego Tea). Her own condition worsens in mid-May, and Victor asks Ann Hobart (Theodore Noyes's favorite) if "I could take care of her when she is sick." Now, however, approval is given because "Theodore and others do not object." By now she measures 37¼ inches at the waist and is in her eighth month. They return to a blissful routine of taking Turkish baths together; Victor washes her hair; they walk in the country to pick wild strawberries. While he works at the Dentist Office, she visits him, and he listens to both her heartbeat and that of the child. "I could hear it quite plain, it beat 109 per minute, hers beat 72." Later that night (June 22), after they had parted, he noticed that there was a light in Mary's room "at 12."

Victor and Mary had journeyed a long way together since the first January night in 1876 when he had "exposed her." Now, she was about to have a child by another man. Whatever mixed emotions he had when he looked at the lighted window he did not record. What he did record was a tragic replay of history. "About 4.AM. Mr Herick came and told me that Marys child was still born at 2:10 A.M. I did not sleep anymore."

Victor had not been allowed to be present at the delivery, but had been called at 6.30 to come down. It was a stillborn birth. Sarah Story, a former member of the Berlin Heights community who had joined in 1872, wrote to Seymour Nash in late June about the birth.

> Dear Mr. Nash,
> Emma says that she promised to write to you as soon as Mary got through but she is so very busy I offered to do it for her.Mary had quite an easy time. Commenced having pain during meeting but stayed till it was out. She had only three or four hard pains and an easy birth but painful it is to think of, her baby was dead. A nice plump little girl

weighing over seven pounds Mary feels badly but behaves beautifully so far. He knows what is best for us, better than we know ourselves.

I am thankful that you was [*sic*] a comfort to Mary when you visited here and wish you could be here during her sickness with your strong spirit to uphold and strengthen her. But God I doubt not will help her to be reconciled to his will. They have asked me to take care of Mary & I pray that I may have a cheerful buoyant spirit that will help her get well in mind and body.

The weather is delightfully cool. Plenty of strawberries.

Your sister

S. A. Story

The Diary of Victor Hawley
November17, 1876–June 23, 1877

Friday November 17, 1876
JO 5½h

Saturday November 18 1876
Mary moved to Mr Joslyn's room to day over the boiler room I got up at 5.40 & went most to Cooks Corners I shot 1 grey and 3 red squirrels.

Sunday November 19 1876
Emma told me that Mary had a hard vomiting & choking time during meeting & sent for Carrie Macknet. Emma told me to call her if Mary had any more trouble I went to her room at 10.45 she did not dare to go to sleep as she would begin to choke I went & told Emma as she was watching with Mrs Hyde with Cornelius Emma asked me stay there & look out for Mary & I could lay down on the bed. I did so Mary slept a little while then wanted some Porridge I got her some after which she did feel the choking so much. Fixing beetles all day

Monday November 20 1876
Mary slept well for 1½h after 5 this morning I slept between 2 & 3 hours. JO 6h Milford gone to Syracuse. With Mary after dinner I got her some grapes which she liked very

much and kept down she throws up everything she is so sick
to her stomach

Tuesday November 21 1876
JO 6h Mary is some better to day but keeps her room

Wednesday November 22 1876
JO 8h Mary has kept her bed all day

Thursday November 23 1876
    JO 6h Mary went down stairs for two or three hours to
day

Friday November 24 1876
    JO 6h Mary came down to the JO for a walk & stopped in
the press room a few minutes she threw up everything when
she got back she was so tired

Saturday November 25 1876
    JO 5h Mary is outdoors some to day with the children.
After dinner I am at work naming my beetles & getting out
duplicates for Geo Dimmock till 6 the practice Telegraphing
for ½ hour with DE Smith he then goes to reading & I go &
see Mary till meeting after meeting I call in & see if she
wants anything.

Sunday November 26 1876
    In Marys room after breakfast for an hour then at the
Seminary till 5.15 then came up & joined the dance in the
Hall. Stayed with the children during meeting Mary asked
me to go to the kitchen with her for some bread & butter &
Alice N. made her some sage tea but it came up she was in
the N. Kitchen most all night after I left her last night. She
did not want me to leave her & *I ought to have stayed in her
room the rest of the night.*

Monday November 27 1876
JO 6h

Tuesday November 28 1876
JO 6h

Wednesday November 29 1876
JO 4h John Freeman came up & called Fredric Marks
about 2.15 A.M. to go & see Martha as her water had broken &
she did not want to be alone. F. called me at 7.30 & I went &
helped him move Martha before breakfast into the room
North of the Green room where Harriet Howard had been

Thursday November 30 1876
Fredric called me at 4 A.M. to go & help Mar tha she gave
birth to a boy at 4.35 A.M. Fredric, Mrs Dunn, Mrs Loveland,
Emma J G.E.C. & I were with her. Dr. C. only 17 minutes
before the birth Martha stood it well for an 8 months
child I told Mary at 5.30 A.M.

Friday December 1 1876
JO 5½h I helped move Mar tha to another bed this morning & back again in the evening

Saturday December 2 1876
JO 6h I took Mary's Wha not from the N. Tower down into
her room.
It has been a sober day with me & my heart aches

Sunday December 3 1876
I was with Mary nearly all day she has had a hard day &
has kept her room most of the time. I lay down on her bed last
evening & slept an hour then we were awake till 3.45 when I
left for my room

Monday December 4 1876
JO 5h I went to the Arcade with Milford about 10 P.M. &
did not go to bed till after 12. Mary slept better last night but
dreamed about me & many other things

Tuesday December 5 1876
JO 5½ I was with Mary till 2 this morning she feels better
to day

Wednesday December 6 1876
JO 6h Mary vomited 4 times today & feels sick to night. I was in her room till 11 last night.

Thursday December 7 1876
JO 6h Mary is some better to day

Friday December 8 1876
JO 6h Setting type & the wind came under the door so cold that I caught cold

Saturday December 9 1876
JO 5h

Sunday December 10 1876
In Marys room till 2 P.M. then went to the Seminary to work on my insects

Monday December 11 1876
JO 5½h

Tuesday December 12 1876
JO 6h

Wednesday December 13 1876
JO 5½h I went down cellar and got some cider in the Arcade in making a syphon of a rubber tube I sucked a strong dose of acetic acid gass into my lungs about 12.30   at 3 P.M. my head began to ache & I quit work

Thursday December 14 1876
JO 5h I feel miserable all day

Friday December 15 1876
JO 2h I lay awake from 12 till 2 this morning then got up & went down into the Nursery Kitchen I was so feverish & my throat was so sore that I got a bowl of ice & eat it I slept a few minutes on the lounge

Saturday December 16 1876
JO 1h I did not sleep any after 2 A.M. I was in Marys room to day & she asked me if I was tempted to go away I told her I would give $50.00 if we were well out of this. both of us had a crying time, but she is with child by T.R.N.

Sunday December 17 1876
I did not go to the Seminary to day   I felt so sick & have to eat ice considerable my throat is so sore and there is some canker in it

Monday December 18 1876
JO 2h Mary has taken to eating lemons & keeps her food down better & she goes out to walk nearly every day

Tuesday December 19 1876
JO 3h Father has said that I shall never have a child by Mary

Wednesday December 20 1876
JO 6h Mary has asked me to stay with others but I cannot

Thursday December 21 1876
Mary in Mr. Jocelyn's room all night. Thank God my heart does not ache so hard to day (JO 5½h)   9 months have nearly past of sorrows & tears with torture & pain, an aching heart that no one knows of & tears would not ease.

Friday December 22 1876
JO 5h Mary has had two vomiting spells since 6 P.M. one after she went to bed after it I rubbed her bowels a few minute & she soon droped of to sleep

Saturday December 23 1876
JO 4h

Sunday December 24 1876
At work on my telegraph instruments enlarging the magnets so that the sounders will work on the main line
Mary is considerable better

Monday December 25 1876
JO 3h I went to the & worked on my instruments from 2 till 6 P.M. Change of Meals Lunch at 8 A.M. Dinner at 10 A.M. Supper at 4 P.M.

Tuesday December 26 1876
JO 3h At the shop working on my Telegraph instuments

Wednesday December 27 1876
JO 6h AS 1h

Thursday December 28 1876
Mary had a hard headache an I put on hot cloths on her head which made her feel better and then I rubbed her forehead a few minutes and she dropped off to sleep after meeting.

Friday December 29 1876
JO 5h Yesterday Milford & I went to Knox corners in a hard snowstorm. We tipped over and it was a long cold ride 7 miles each way & the horse had to walk most of the way. We went to see Mr Kelmer.

Saturday December 30 1876
JO 4h

Sunday December 31 1876
I slept with Mary last night *had* connection. L.B. has not felt as well since the change of meals. I went to the Carpenters shop and worked on my Telegraph instruments.

Memoranda
(SH) ride 9 ironers Aug 21, 1862 to Casinova Lake
Dennis Shaw Colchester Vt
Charles H Lyman Gericho Vt
CC Chadwich Jeffersonville Vt
C Durt Clinton
Mr Curtis Utica
D.A. Marcy. W. Union Tel. Syracuse

Mar 28, 1876 P.O. Order Payable to H.H. Babcock $5.00
   No 11 Eighteenth St Chicago Ill Sent by R.V.
Hawley
   HO Houghton & Co $17.50 Riverside Press Cambridge Mass
      FN 392 Chapel St.
   NY Aquarium Corner of 35st & Broadway public

   Box Telegraph Inst. ex. 40 *Charged to Entomology Bill*
   4 Rubber Tubes
   ½ lb #32 Sk. c. magnet wire @ 1.95 =   2.62

	.97
	3.59

Memoranda

		Dolls Cts
Feb 14	Mending Shoes	.15
Feb 16	Mending coat & pants	.78
Jaf 25	7 Boxes Colars @ 14	.98
	New Pants	6.90
	Hat	2.25
	Cloth Shoes	1.75
	Slips	1.75
	Rubber 630	.55
	Satchel 5.50	
April 11	½ doz Oranges	.18
	Mendin Vest & Pants	.45
Jan	Mask	.25
April	SJC	.28
April 6	2 Neckties .13 & .17	.30
May 18	Hat Band	.09
May 26	½ Doz @ .56 M Stockins No. 10 ½	3.32
		19.98
May 30	Mending Shoes	1.80
June 1	" Pants	.30
Aug	" Coat & "	
Aug	Tooth Pick Holder	.15
Oct 7	Cloth Gaiters	2.00
Oct	4 lbs Powder @ .35 =	1.40
	9 lbs Shot @ .10	.90
		2.30

Cash Account—January	Received	Paid
on hand	4.01	
Mr Haley		1.68
PB	1.68	
8	Otis	20.49
Ex		.86
12	Doz Eggs	3.60
11	Wages	7.26
15	"	7.09
22	Office	21.95
"	Wages	1.00
"	"	5.00
24	Eggs	6.37
Office	10.00	
27	Jack MacQ	5.00
"	Annie Burk	3.25
30	Mrs Stephens	3.25

Cash Account—February		
5	Wages	4.21
6	Mrs Stephens	2.00
20	" "	5.25
22	Milford	1.00
23	" Nuts	.40
25	" Furs	1.75
	1.35	

Cash Account—October	Received	Paid
30	6 Insulated H	1.20

Cash Account—December		
	Clarence	
	"	1.27
	373	
	69	
	305	
	75	
	230	

Diary of R.V. Hawley
January 1, 1877–June 23, 1877

J O 5h

Monday January 1 1877

I made some tea for Mary after meeting & after she drank it I went to the kitchen & drank some, then sat by the stove & worked on my telegraph instruments till 1 this morning. She said she laid awake until nearly 1 A.M. If I had known it I would have gone to her room (where Mr Joslyn used to room) and wished her a happy new year

J Office 5h

Tuesday January 2 1877

I slept with Mary last night as she did not feel well & I had to wake her up every few minutes as she slept hard & was quite feverish till we had connection at 5 A.M. after which she slept better

Milford said that Annie Kelly was to be Dentist I told him that LF Dunn & E F Hutchins used to say that Annie did not have good enough eyesight for a Dentist.

Job Office 5h AL

Wednesday January 3 1877

Slept with Mary no connection we cuddled down and slept as of old although she was not well but feverish & had the headache all day yesterday & went to bed as soon as she had got through giving the children their breakfast. Today she went up into Emma & changed rooms with Mary Smith as it was so noisy by her room over the boilers

JO6h

Thursday January 4 1877

Mary is quite nervous & has the headache she was not dressed yestuerday or to day but has to keep her bed most of the time. I sent for some organges & she eats one or two every day as lemons are too sour for her now she has eaten them after her meals to keep from vomiting

J O5h

Friday January 5 1877

I moved into the N. Tower & Clarence has gone back into the Tontine Mary is better and was dressed today

Daniel Abbott who been in the Job Office for [SH] has asked me once or twice why I did not go into the Dentistry again   I told him it was because I was not asked to.

Milford has asked me about the business & has said that he would not like pulling teeth &c but since has said that perhaps he should be a Dentist

JO6h

Saturday Jan 6 1877

Mr Hamilton had some talk with Milford this forenoon privately & I thought that it might have been about my going back into the Dentist Office but during the day he asked me if I could get along without him four days in the week, I supposed so although I wanted him to stay in the printing with me another year. He talked to me so about his leaving the J.O. that I could hardly eat my dinner at 4 P.M. & Mary came up to the Towers & I had a long time crying I felt so it made me feel sich at heart & I was pale

Sunday Jan 7 1877

Mary gone back to her room today   I slept with Mary in Emma' room or rather with Herbert in Emma's bed & I feel better this morning whilst changing beds in the Tower   Mr Hamilton came up & asked me to go into the Dentist Office to work   I said I would & asked if Mr Noyes wished it   he said it was Theodores move but he would see Mr Noyes about it. He spoke to him and then told me that Mr Noyes was glad to have me take the buisiness again

JO6 ¾h

Monday Jan 8 1877

Printing the Fruit Labels it is my last days work in the Job Office printing Lima Bean Labels 1500 of them Tryphenas funeral Mary has come back to her room today as she feels better but not very strong yet

Dentist Office 6 hours
Tuesday Jan 9 1877
At work on Celuloid plate and packing a new vulcanizer
that is to be sent back to B.D.M.Co. I am in Marys room writing the last few pages she has gone to bed & is fast asleep at
10.30 P.M. I have read to her from the Testament for an hour
every day for some time back. Father said that Martha said
she thought I ought to be happy now that I had gone into the
Tower & D.O. I told him I did feel happier than I was a spell
ago.

DO6h
Wednesday January 10 1877

DO6h
Thursday January 11 1877

DO6h
Friday January 12 1877
Slept with M [scratched out]
A talk from W C read to night on stirpiculture and it
made me feel so that I cried in M after meeting

DO6h
Saturday January 13 1877
Slept with Mary bath at the window in the morning
Vulcanizing a plate for Mr Inslie & fixing John Nortons
teeth drilled out an amalgam filling that E F Hutchins put in
between two gold fillings hitting both and creating cemical
reaction that made the tooth ache

Sunday Jan 14 1877
At work putting in my wires from the battery to my instru ments and a larger wire to D E Smiths room on insula-
tors Mary has put on a new dress to night I danced one set
with Olive Ann to night Father sleeps in the Tower as
Roswell is lame. Father asked me if I wanted a baby now   I
told him I had rather not have one now, he said that there
was so much turmoil in the Com munity that he did not want

his children to have any now Little does he know how I feel at not having one by Mary. He has made my life bitter & I am far from happy

DO6h
Monday January 15 1877
I commenced milling off Mr Inslie plate and broke it, then I melted some wax and rolled it out into sticks for waxing plates. I have cooked Mary some oysters for her supper for a few nights back and she says they are real good and keeps them down.

DO7 ¼h
Tuesday January 16 1877
Making a cast & waxing a model for Mr Inslie an under plate. Mary lay down on her bed & would not go to bed when I was in the room as she has done when I was there for some time past. I had commenced practicing writing & told her I would turn my back so as not to see her but she would not go to bed, so I soon left without biding her good night Myron has left the Community.

DO6½h
Wednesday January 17 1877
Vulcanizing Mr Inslies plate. Mary came up to see me just as I was getting up. She said she did not sleep any before 12 oclock because I left her so, after dinner last night we both had a crying time & I could not read the Testament without crying. Myron kept Mary from going away with me & now he has left. I left her & went down into the Nussery Kitchen & saw Mrs hall & then went back at 12.30 & stayed till 2 this morning   Sweet was the time

D.O.6½h
Thursday January 18 1877
Filling a tooth for Mrs Burnham & polishing Mr Inslie plate. Mary went to bed last night at 6.30 as she was sleepy & her head ached some I made her some egg nog about 7 P.M. she sewed too much but today she feels better. I cooked some

oysters & took to her room for her supper tonight She is now
sewing on her babys double gown at 10.30 P.M. whilst I am
writing I am watchman to night & was last night for Roswell

DO6 ¼h
Friday January 19 1877
Articulating & waxing an upper plate for Mr Inslie. I was
in Agusta's room & Mary went & cooked her oysters to night.
I had to run the Boilers to night till G.W. Hamilton came
home from Utica. Herbert is sleeping with Mary they have
just gone to bed at 9.30 & I am going to rub her hips & legs as
they ache they did not stop aching so I went to bed with her &
had connection & the pain all left her.

DO 6½h
Saturday January 20 1877
Putting Mr I plate into the flash & boiling it & screwing
it together to squeeze the celuloid into shape. Mary said this
forenoon that the pains were all gone. After she took a Turkish bath to day they came on again and she is quite lame this
evening. I sent to her but she declined as she did not go to
sleep till 2 AM & is tired & sleepy after giving the children a
tea party

Sunday January 21 1877
I took my telegraph line from Sidneys room (as he has
gone to W.C.) & put it on to the Office building last night &
this morning I run the wire to the main line battery. I cleaned
Mary's closet, took her summer dresses up garret & swept her
room which took till 3.30 then I went to dinner then practiced
dancing at the Children's Play House then run boilers for ½
hour then danced with Olive Ann in the Hall. I came to
Marys room at 3.15 A M & went to bed & had connection. We
had not slept but little

DO6 ¼h
Monday January 22 1877
Polishing Mr I plate then I went to the Mill & turned
some wooden spindles for D.O. grind stones

DO6½h
Tuesday January 23 1877
At work on Mrs Tow ners plate   I went to Mary's room at
2.30 A.M. & went to bed, we did not have connection & I have
felt bad all day & cried 3 times this evening

DO6 ¼h
Wednesday January 24 1877
An Amalgam filling for Mary Baker & one for Phoebe
Sibly
This has been a sober day for me. Shall I ever be happy
here. Oh why this turmoil of life it would be happiness if I
could have a baby by Mary but now it is misery & hope with
out hope or hope long deferred, but I pray God to help me

DO3h
Thursday January 25 1877
Fixing a filling for Phoebe & setting corundrum wheels
till noon then went to W.P. & worked on my telegraph magnets till 5.35 when I got home Mary was in Mr Seymours lap
she had a fainting turn but did not quite faint away her food
troubled her I slept with her last night & feel brighter & she
felt well this morning she has changed rooms with Arthur
Towner for tonight & I take care of Mrs Higgins to night

DO6½h
Friday January 26 1877
1 Gold Filling & 2 Amalgam & 1 os artificial for F A
Marks 2 A for Mr Ackley   Communication with Mary at 7
P.M.

Sunday January 28 1877
At work finishing my telegraph instruments in Mary's
room and after meeting putting Edsons instrument on to another stand & making connections   I danced with Phoebe
then with Carrie Boles this evening
Herbert asked his mother if I would make him some egg
nog so I did this morning when I made Mary's but he threw it
up. I came down at 5 A.M. & went to bed with Mary.

DO6½h
Monday January 29 1877
2 Amalgam filling & 1 Gold

After dinner I connected our Tower line with the W.P. Battery & line & my instruments work well. Mary talked to Mr Seymour about some of the men being weak towards their children as well as their mothers Mr said she was thinking evil, she said she was not & talked quite earnestly & sincerely to him last night & he did not stay with her as he spoke of doing she feels bad that he should do so

DO6 ¼h
Tuesday January 30 1877
Mary measures 35½ in

Getting & packing my bag for E.F. Hutchins to take Dentist tools &c to W.C. She & Carrie Macknet left for W.C. this evening I commenced practicing telegraphing with Edson to night at 6 P.M. Mary was quite sober after her talk & she had a crying time last night

Mr Towner & Martin went to Syracuse to see Myron then came home & talked with Mr Noyes then Martin went to Syracuse again

DO6 ¼h
Wednesday January 31 1877
2A for Mr Geoff & 1G for Emma I slept with Mary last night & this morning at 4.45 I went to the kitchen & got her a tumbler of milk after drinking it she went to sleep & slept most of the time till 7.10 & then got up as she waits on the children at breakfast. She thought she looked younger this morning. She was tired and went to bed about 6 P.M. I took her knitting away from her & she lay down on the bed

DO6½h
Thursday February 1 1877
Mrs Clark 1 h Emma 1 G & cleaning Mary feels bright to night & is sewing after meeting her fine night dress for her baby that is to come I lay down on her bed for an hour last night after meeting with my hand on her I felt the baby move

3 or four times after she went to sleep & the night before I felt it 10 or 12 times before I went to sleep. She has a cold to night. Mary is 4½ m long & measures 34¾ in

6¼h DO
Friday February 2 1877
2G for Emma

Saturday February 3 1877
Cleaning tools & polishing them to take off rust formed by E F H having the nitric acid bottle open near them.
3 G for Emma

DO6¼h
Sunday February 4 1877
Swept Mary's room   I danced with Mary Smith in the evening

DO6¼h
Monday February 5 1877
At work on Mrs V Velzer's plate
I commenced waiting on the table this morning.

DO7h
Tuesday February 6 1877
At work on Mrs Velzer's plate vulcanized it during dinner hour

D.O. 6¼h
Wednesday February 7 1877
Finished Mrs Van's upper plate
I saw Mrs M Hall in the N. Kitchen at 11.15 & slept with Mary, she has felt quite well all day better than usual & we both slept well

D.O.2h
Thursday February 8 1877
Malleting for L F Dunn &c. he put in 3 small Gold fillings for Mrs Newhouse in about ¾ of an hour 7 he put in an amalgam filling for me in about ½ h. I have a hard cold & it was

hard work to stand up when striking for L.F.D. who puts in fillings by the old method. After he left I lay down on the lounge for 2 hours & sweat some with the room at 90° took a T. Bath. Mary had me soak my feet & drink some composition tea & go to bed wraped in a woolen blanket

DO½h
Friday February 9 1877
Mary came to the DO after breakfast. Asked LFD if it was good for me to eat cracker as much as I do &c. I went to bed in my room. she got a freestone & put it to my feet & gave me some hot lemonade & put warm woolen blankets around me. I sweat for 2½ hours Clarence sponged me off & rubbed me with a warm towel about 2.30 P.M. After dinner Mary said that Emma spoke to her about our being together so much that GEC said it would be worse for us in the future. Most likely LFD has been making a fuss, because she was at the DO & he was seen talking with GEC afterwards

DO4h
Saturday February 10 1877
Waxing plate for Mrs Velzer I was at the DO all day but did not feel like working so lay on the lounge part of the time.
Emma spoke to me about Mary & I being together so much that it was causing some talk   I told I would try & not disturb folks.
I suppose that LFD hates to have Mary come to the Dentist Office

Sunday February 11 1877
I was intending to work on my insects to day but my cold holds on so that I cannot afford to work on them so I fixed a ground wire from my coil to the Office line, then spent the afternoon in Mary's room. I have lost 6½ lbs. in the last three days my weight is now 135 lbs

DO6½h
Monday February 12 1877
At work on Mrs Velzers plate got it into the lower half of the flash to night. I read a story to Mary from the Galaxy.

"Applied Science." Herbert slept with mary and she went to bed as meeting but did not go to sleep as Herbert was playing on the bed. After meeting I read to her till 10 oclock.

DO6h
Tuesday February 13 1877
Vulcanized Mrs Velzers under plate   J H Barron was in the D.O. nearly all day   I finished reading "Applied Science" to night then

DO6h
Wednesday February 14 1877
Polished Mrs Velzers under plate

DO6½h
Thursday February 15 1877
2 Gold Fillings for Emma.

DO6¼h
Friday February 16 1877
Preparing a cavity in upper right molar for Mary Baker & cleaning teeth.

DO2½h
Saturday February 17 1877
Changed Mary's beadstead so that she can get into bead easier
I slept with Mary last night

Sunday February 18 1877
I swept Mary's room she does not feel well to day as she did not sleep but little for two nights. Mr Seymour slept with her last nigh
I watched Mr Higgins the last half of the night & he died about 8.15 P.M.
Mary did not get up till 11.30 A.M. About 1 P.M. I went down & cooked her some tenderloin &c.

DO6½h
Monday February 19 1877
Mary feels better to day & went up to my room & looked over my clothes with me to see how many I have got to have for the year.

Marys baby moved so strong that I could see it move the bed clothes, a sheet, woolen blanket a bed quilt & spread after she had gone to bed I could see the motions of the child above all the clothes   She is 5 months along.

DO
Tuesday February 20 1877
Mary is quite smart to day & is sewing to night at 9.30   She went to a Stereop ticon exebition in the Hall this evening Centennial Scenes.

Mary measures 36 inches to night & I could see the baby move the clothes to night. I stayed with Mary a little while to night at 10 P.M.

DO6½h
Wednesday February 21 1877

DO6¼h
Thursday February 22 1877
Mary did not sleep well for two nights & the noise from the boiler room disturbed her & she has gone into Emmas room to sleep

DO6¾h
Friday February 23 1877

DO5h
Saturday February 24 1877
N E Dris Ba.A Teacher & Howard G Thompson called on me this after noon from the Castle the later bought a Partridge egg & a Meadow Larks egg @ 10 cts each

Sunday February 25 1877
At work in the lower room at the Seminary with Cornelius, he is papering a large case for his animals & I am

getting out duplicate beetles to send Geo. Dimmock of Mass I have not worked at my insects for some time till yestuerday I worked on them from four till six. I run the Boilers for G.W.H. during the dance. The women chose partners I had time to dance with Emma; & Constance.

DO6½
Monday February 26 1877

Mary went to bed after waiting on the children at dinner as she was tired she eat some Graham mush at noon & it seems to take all her strength to digest it. She lay on her bed with Herbert during meeting. I got her some milk to drink after meeting & she has gone to bed in Emma's room where she has slept for a few nights. She came & asked me to get her some milk last night after she had gone to bed & I had also.

DO6½h
Tuesday February 27 1877

Waiting on the table at breakfast & then to the Dentist Office till 3 P.M. After dinner go to the Seminary to work on my beetles till 6 then practice telegraphing with D Edson Smith for ½ hour. then read the Testament to Mary till meeting time. She took a walk with Mr Seymour after dinner

DO6½h
Wednesday February 28 1877

Mary came to the N Tower to sleep as Roswell is off. She was cold after going to bed her bowels were bloated so from wind & the baby that she was in considerable pain so I let on the steam & she sat up for some time but finely went to bed but did not get to sleep till about 12.40 this morning She went to bed during meeting to night.

DO6¼h
Thursday March 1 1877

Mary does not feel very well to night but has done her work to day.

DO6¼h
Friday March 2 1877

DO6¼h
Saturday March 3 1877

DO1½h
Sunday March 4 1877
At work at the Seminary with Cornelius. He is fixing a new case of animals.

I took Marys feather bed from Emma's Room down to her room this morning as she is going back to her own room to sleep.

DO6¼h
Sunday March 5 1877
Through waiting on the table.[SH]
I slept with Mary

DO6h
Tuesday March 6 1877

DO6½h
Wednesday March 7 1877

DO 6¾h
Thursday March 8 1877
I mad Mary's egg nog this morning & did not see her again till she came to the Seminary after dinner where Cornelius & I were at work she asked me to go to walk with her but it was rainy so I did not go. We went to the Bible lecture in the evening & had our Bible reading after meeting.

DO 7¼h
Friday March 9 1877
[SH] 2 large Gold Fillings for Mr Thayer.
Tableaus of Cleopatra to night in the Hall
Mary went to bed soon after meeting & we did not have our Bible reading to night.

DO5h
Saturday March 10 1877

Sunday March 11 1877
At work on beetles in the lower room at the Seminary. I was dancing with Mrs Marks this even ing & Mary was sitting near looking on when Herbert ran & put his hands against her bowels so hard that she could hardly bre athe or keep from crying. She went to bed with her feet & legs as cold as ice I put warm blanket around her & some hot flats to her feet & I slept some on the bed with my clothes on during the night.

DO5h
Monday March 12 1877
Mary did not get up till 12.30 to day she is getting along well but has to keep quiet after waiting on the children at 1 till 2 she went to bed & I brought her breakfast & supper to her

DO6½h
Tuesday March 13 1877
Mary feels better to day and we hope her baby has not been hurt by Herbert.

DO6¼h
Wednesday March 14 1877
I slept with Mary last night as Roswell wanted the Tower Room & she feels quite well to day & says that I have been a help to her.

DO6¾h
Thursday March 15 1877

DO6¹₂H
Friday March 16 1877
Roswell went to Syra cuse & did not expect to come back last night so Mary came to my room to sleep as it was stiller there but Roswell came home at midnight & I sent him to her room.

I have got the tooth ache this afternoon & looked for LF
Dunn but he was at Oneida it grew easier about 5 P.M. I took
a hot flat to bed to keep my face warm.

Saturday March 17 1877
I went to Oneida & had my tooth pulled to day. I took gas
the first breath I could taste it & the third I felt at the bottom
of my lungs & the fourth or fifth I felt a slight prickling sen-
sation down my legs to my toes & every thing seem dark & I
was asleep. When I awoke from the darkness Mr Smith told
me to spit, the tooth was out he asked me if I had not quite a
strong con stitution as it took 1½ dose of gas to put me to
sleep I breathed easily & did not make any noise the tooth
broke all to pieces and he had to use 3 instru ments to get it
all out. I opened and shut my mouth after the tooth broke &
the cork droped out & shut my mouth so tight they had to
work to get it open, but I did not feel anything when the tooth
was pulled.

DO₁h

Sunday March 18 1877
At work on beetles after sweeping Mary's room. Did not
dance as Mary does not feel well tonight   I got some lunch for
her tonight

DO6½h

Monday March 19 1877
Mary has gone to bed & I have been writing down items
for the past week since tending a rehersal of Pickwick in
which I take the part of Snodgrass.

DO6h

Tuesday March 20 1877
Mary has given up waiting on the children at their meals
& works in the waiters room. She has had to shew others her
work to day & working in the waiters room has been hard for
her to day.

DO6h
Wednesday March 21 1877

DO6½h
Thursday March 22 1877

DO6h
Friday March 23 1877

Tuesday March 27 1877
Mary has had to quit work in the waiters room as she feels as though she had given away so much life to the children that she needs a rest.

DO6h
Wednesday March 28 1877
Father left for W.C. to night with Ann Hobert. I did not see him when he left as Mr Jones was talking so to Mary that it made her very nervous & she had a hard crying spell.

DO6h
Thursday March 29 1877
Mr Jones talked with Mary till she got very nervous so she slept in the North Tower with me so as to have a quiet place to sleep.

DO4h
Friday March 30 1877

Saturday March 31 1877
My face has troubled me some so I went to Oneida to see Mr Smith. I got ½ Doz Bananas for Mary she had thrown up her dinner. She said they were good. I got some ham but she would not eat it as she had talked with Carrie A Macknet who told her to pray about it.

Sunday April 1 1877
I danced with Maria Barron, Mrs Skinner, Rosamond, & Mary Whatley. The last dance for the season. Emma talked so

to Mary about her working that she had a crying time, & has thrown up her supper. Mrs Marks gave me some beer so I asked her for some for Mary & she gave me some. Mary liked it. I glued in some corn pith for insect boxes.

Monday April 2 1877
Mary is changing rooms with Martha as it is so noisy she cannot sleep well. I helped clean Marys room & Martha has got all moved but the carpet is taken up & Marys things are in baskets. Abby Burnham, Mrs Kelly & Emma are helping move & clean. Mary has thrown up her food 2 or 3 times so (Tuesday) night she had some ham & eggs. I got the ham Satuerday but she did not dare to eat it as she had spoken to C A Macknet.

Tuesday April 3 1877
I took out the windows from the lying in room where Mary is going so they could clean them & helped put down the carpet. I spoke to Geo E Cra gin & he had Dr Carpenter see Mary as she wanted to see him. He told her her food was not nourishing her, that must not over do & get tired but go out and take the air in the forenoon & he would send something to help her. She had some ham &c.

DO1½h
Wednesday April 4 1877
I went to Oneida & had a tooth filled
Mary has got settled and had a criticism to day at 11   Mr E H Hamilton said this morning she might have a whole pig if she wanted. Constance is going to make her egg nog so this is my last time this morning she has 2 eggs most of the time but now only wants one. Mr Herrick is to wait on her in my place so I must step out of the way.

DO6½h
Thursday April 5 1877
Mary feels better as she has kept her food down for 2 days & she sleeps better in her new room, Constance slept in her room Monday night & Carrie Macknet sleeps in the room

with her now in another bed. D. Edson Smith took 20 words a minute when we were prac ticing telegraphing to night for 15 minutes 408 words. Theodore Noyes has come

DO7h
Friday April 6 1877
Dr Carpenters medicine has come for Mary. I finished reading the Testament to Mary to day. I have read from 5 till 6 for a few days some of the time I read to her from 6.30 till 7.20. She asked me what made me so sober it is Theodores coming & thoughts of what passed a year ago. I have to smother my feelings as much as I can so she will not see the tears. Oh God help me such an aching heart.

DO6½h
Saturday April 7 1877
Mr Herrick goes in to see Mary after meeting & I have only seen her but a few minu tes as meeting was out.

Sunday April 8 1877
At work on beetles all day till 4 Then went into the East meadow with Fredric Marks to try shooting with Milfords Pocket Rifle that has a telescope on it. I was late to the dance but danced once with Emma.

DO4h
Monday April 9 1877
After dinner I went over to the new barn with Humphreys class of boys to get some corn pith to put into Insect cases. We did not get back in time for the boys to go to their meeting. Cornelius brought up a white squirrel from A P Cleveland to put with our grey one. Theodore proposes to have the W.C. family come here to live.

DO6¼h
Tuesday April 10 1877

DO6h
Wednesday April 11 1877

DO6½h
Thursday April 12 1877

DO6h
Saturday April 14 1877
I made egg nog for Mary & handed it to Emma.

Sunday April 15 1877
I printed some figures to No. my beetles with & put on some of them. In the evening I danced with Mrs. Marks, Mrs. Skinner, Cossette & Mrs. Easton.

I asked Mrs Skinner to ask Mary to come to my room tonight but Mrs Skin ner would not ask her and said she was afraid my influence would be bad for Mary & draw her down into a sickley state They think the separ ation is what has helped Mary but it is the change of rooms & the medicine which Dr Carpenter sent her which has stoped the Leaccaped & throwing up phlem, & chewing spruce gum has enabled her to swallow the saliva which she had to spit it out. Theodore has gone to W.C. James Hatch has come from W.C. Daniel & I went over to muck shed & set in the hand car wheels but it runs hard yet

Friday April 20 1877
I have not felt well for a few days so Mary has made me some bitters of Balmany to drink

Saturday April 21 1877
Milford has gone to Joppa & I wait on 3 tables for him till he comes back.

Sunday April 22 1877
I waited on tables for Milford I printed some figures to No. my beetles with & put on a few [scratched out]. I the evening I danced. Mary went to walk with me over past the muck shed I found a Star nosed Mole floating down the brook nerly drowned. No. beetles at the Seminary. Cornelius put in the glass front to the Animal case. About 2 P.M. Mary went to the Printing Office with me. I set some figures.

Monday April 23 1877

Setting figures before breakfast. Waited on three tables for Mil ford. After dinner I carried a spring bed to Marys room and made her bed as she does not feel well she feels weak & exhausted but has waited on the children & kept school today. She went to bed but got up & went to supper then went to bed before meeting. I got her some ice water for the night.

Saturday May 12 1877

Mary had some pain it may be an ague pain but she said that it one of the forerunners, some like the ones she had before the birth of her other child.

Sunday May 13 1877

Arthur Towner & I went on to the west hill after Plants & Insects I shot 3 birds for Cornelius

I have commenced making Marys egg nog in the morning again. I make some for Harriet Howard

Monday May 14 1877

Mary has had 2 or 3 more pains.

Thursday May 17 1877

Mary asked Ann if I could help take care of her when she is sick.

Friday May 18 1877

Carrie Macknet has gone to W C with Ann Hobert & Theodore. Carrie roomed in Marys room & Mary was sorry to have her go

Saturday May 19 1877

Mary is feeling quite well for her but does not do much work as it will not do for her to get tired

Sunday May 20 1877

Arthur Towner, Clar ence & I went to the lake. We started at 8.15 & went via Oneida Vally, reached Fish Creek 3.30 Collected Plants, Birds & Insects on the way. Clarence &

I went in swimming in the lake We 3 took supper & started for home at 5.45 via Liste Bridge reached home 9.20

Monday May 21 1877

After dinner Corn elius & Henry Hunter skin ned the birds Clarence & I shot & I pinned out the beetles I got yestuer day, then Henry helped put in some corn pith into some boxes

Mary said that Mrs Dunn came & told her that I could help take care of her as Theodore & others do not object to it. Mary is 37¼ inches round her waist

Sunday June 10 1877

I took a Turkish Bath with Mary & gave her a good shampooing after meeting

Tuesday June 12 1877

I picked some wild strawberrys and gave to Mary

Thursday June 14 1877

Mary got some strawberrys of Rosa mond & we eat them after meeting.

I called Mr Herrick for Hellen Miller she could not sleep about 11.45 I took some Insects into the Turkish Bath to dry during meeting.

Wednesday June 20 1877

I have received some insects & birds eggs from W.C. they came in a chartered freight car with furniture &c.

After dinner I went to the Larch grove & caught some butter flies.

Thursday June 21 1877

I gave Mary a bath after meeting in the Childrens dressing Room Bath Room. I finished writing names of the butterflies in my new case after dinner in Marys room. The case is going into the Bird Room in the Seminary.

Friday June 22 1877

Filling Emily Otis tooth. Mary came to the Dentist Office.

About 6 P.M. Mary asked me to see if I could hear the babys heart beat, I could quite plain, it beat 109 per minute hers beat 72 ten minutes after the babies beat 112 per minute.

About 11 Lilly Hobart heard the babys heart beat.

I went and got some leaves for my silk worms about 11 . There was a light in Marys room at 12.

Saturday June 23 1877

About 4 A.M. Mr Herick came and told me that Marys child was still born at 2.10 . . I did not sleep any more. After a while Lilly came and told then Emma then Fidelia who asked me to come down it was 6.30

13. Theodore Noyes, 1873.
Courtesy Oneida Community Mansion House.

14. Harriet Holton Noyes.
Courtesy Oneida Community Mansion House.

15. Oneida Community train depot, 1870s.
Courtesy Arents Collection, Bird Library, Syracuse University.

16. Wallingford Community factory, ca. 1878.
Courtesy Arents Collection, Bird Library, Syracuse University.

17. Turkish bath, Oneida Community, 1870s.
Courtesy Arents Collection, Bird Library, Syracuse University.

18. Wicker bench, Oneida Community, 1870s.
Courtesy Arents Collection, Bird Library, Syracuse University.

19. Young women of the Oneida Community, 1860.
Courtesy Oneida Community Mansion House.

20. Woman of the Oneida Community nursing child, 1870s.
Courtesy Oneida Community Mansion House.

21. Community members with children at the gazebo, 1870s.
Courtesy Arents Collection, Bird Library, Syracuse University.

22. Oneida Community children in buckboard, 1870s.
Courtesy Oneida Community Mansion House.

23. Horse and trap, 1880s.
Courtesy Oneida Community Mansion House.

 CHAPTER FIVE

Try It Over Again

*It would seem as though the physical struc-
ture of future generations was almost as
plastic as clay, under the control of the
breeder's will.*
—Francis Galton,
Hereditary Talent and Character (1865)

ather than being broken by the ordeal, Mary Jones
emerged with her spirit intact and determined to pursue an independent course unchecked. Victor's diary entries
for the next week set the framework for the struggle that was
ahead. "I spoke to Theodore about Marys adopting a baby. He
said he would see Father about it . GEC asked Mary how did
she feel. she said real smart. I am ready to get up & try it
over again." "A letter was read in meeting from Dr Carpenter
& one from Mr Noyes that said Mary ought not to have a
baby." Mr. Towner and Mrs. Leonard told Mary and I that it
was decided in meeting that Mary could not have another
child." Her willingness and eagerness to "get up and try it
over again" was, of course, a challenge to the community. And
it responded quickly.

Within a week after Mary's remark to George Cragin that
she wanted to "start again," the community physician, an elder leader, and a community meeting all agreed that she
should not have a child. This unanimity of sentiment did not
emerge solely out of a desire to suppress Mary's willful de-

175

sires but was also generated by a genuine concern that the childbearing process would be injurious to her health. On a deeper level, however, her assertion of her rights represented a significant threat to the authority structure within the colony. Her wanting to start over again emphasized her continuing commitment to her "excessive" desire to have a child—possibly with Victor—but one that would serve her own needs rather than those of the community.

Sarah Story continued her correspondence with Edwin Nash about Mary's condition, observing that Mary was no longer behaving "beautifully," as reported in the letter of late June, but had taken an independent and anticommunity attitude:

> Dear Mr.Nash:
> Your note came in due time & I was glad to hear from you. And now I will tell you the /disagreeable things first, though I much regret that I have anything unpleasant to tell you. You know I told you that Mary behaved well & said she thought the community had been very kind to her all through and had done what they could, but the second day after the child was born she told G.E.Craigin that she was ready to try again. This surprised us all very much & I said to her in a kind way, Mary? that is a great deal to go through and not have a living child. so she sticks to the point with a tenacity that is astonishing.

Jones had reacted in an "astonishing manner" because her tenacity represented her assertion to possess a child contrary to community sentiment. Mary Jones was thinking about herself and had an "inordinate" desire to have a child. Story's letter to Nash examines that desire:

> She replied, I think that I could have a living child. So you see she sticks to the point with a tenacity that is astonishing. So Dr.C. Talked with Mr.Noyes & Dr.Carpenter about it who both decided that it is not best under the circumstances for her to try again. Though Mr.Noyes left it up for the family to decide. so we had the subject up in meeting to settle forever the question. Shall Mary bear children?

The question was an important one, not just because it bore on the Hawley-Jones liaison, but because it dealt directly with the emergence of individualistic attitudes that challenged the colony's supremacy on certain central issues; however, the question was too narrowly defined to challenge community authority. "Shall Mary bear children? And run the risk of bringing sickly children into the community, after we have taken the foremost rank in stirpiculture." The community voted unanimously that it was best for her never to try again. Sarah Story had sympathy for Mary but sided with the community on both scientific and moral grounds. "I am sorry that Mary feels so, but I should be sorry indeed to have weakly, sickly children brought into the world. Indeed I think that it would be wicked in God's sight to do so. I suppose you will get a full account of all this in the journal."

All this in July 1877 just two years before the community broke up. The basis for the community refusal to allow Mary Jones to have another child was a mixture of biblical and scientific assumptions. Those assumptions were, in 1877 wearing thin, despite the unanimity of the colony decision. Mary's declaration that "she was ready to try it over again" was a defiant statement that did not sit well with the community elders. Here was a "sickly" woman asserting her right to maternity, her right to control her destiny, her right to a child of her own. Her rebellion was closely linked to her relations with Victor, and so he received a talking-to from the colony elders, who insisted that he "separate from her." At that moment Victor and Mary were wedded in their defiance of community rule and purpose. They wanted a child and were prepared to have one inside or outside of Oneida. "She [Mary] talked with Mr.Towner & told him that she was ready to leave the community. So am I with her."

Despite their rebelliousness and clear statements about their intentions, the previous nine months had taken a great deal out of them. Mary's sickness and Victor's melancholia returned after the pregnancy had ended tragically. During early July she had lost weight and was now down to ninety-two pounds. In mid-July the colony made another effort to keep them apart; Victor was asked once again to stop caring for her. Colony members had gone to James Towner with the complaint that Victor was more of a hindrance than a help. The news so disturbed him that he could not eat or sleep and he began his lamentation once again. "Oh how my heart aches from the separation."

What now follows is a struggle among Mary, Victor, and the community. At this point the community has written off Victor as a nuisance, a malcontent, someone without whom it would be better off. Its attitude toward Mary is more benign and complex because there is still the hope that she can be brought back to the fold if she is kept away from Victor's negative influences.

Late in July, when Mary and Victor's sister Emma go on a trip to Auburn, Victor feels abandoned. As her carriage leaves the grounds he thinks, "Do you love the community better than me?" That the answer may be "yes" makes it impossible for him to work, and he is forced to brood on the fact that "tis the third time she has gone from me thus and left me to stand the storm alone." With her departure Victor is thrown into a state of absolute despair; sleep evades him, and he launches into more soliloquies. "Come back today my dear Mary & take me of tomorrow, to lead a happy life free from this place of sorrow. In a cottage dear without these tears, a happy life we'll lead tomorrow." Drowning in bathos and self-pity, he is confused about work, about her reasons for taking the trip, about his own fate.

His fate is decided for him on July 30 when he is called before a six-member committee for an offense against colony standards. The last straw has nothing to do with Mary Jones; rather, it comes because he gave a third glass of brandy to young Phoebe Allen when she came to the Dentist Office, and it made her sick. The committee takes him out of the Dentist Office. Speaking for the committee, Erastus Hamilton informs him that "the community had had forebearance long enough. . . . No other work was given me . . . . Evidently the whole move & purport of the meeting was to have us go." Mary is still away, and other colony members try to dissuade him from leaving immediately because after the committee meeting, he began making plans to depart. On August 2 he leaves Oneida, noting that the "parting was severe for a little

while." He goes to Syracuse and takes up residence at a
boarding establishment, Talbott House.

Having left Oneida, Victor is faced with the problem of
work and so begins making the rounds of dental offices in
Syracuse and the vicinity. In the meantime Mary has returned to the colony, and Victor waits, in agony, to hear from
her. "Oh Mary Mary why don't you answer my letters." After
a week in Syracuse, he does get a letter, but it is devastating;
she has changed her mind. "I got a letter from Mary in which
she says she will stay in the community & will not go out
with me. O God why am I thus forsaken. It is a bitter day to
me and my heart bleeds and tears rool down my face to the
page I write to here at Oneida." Whether she had been convinced to stay by Emma Hawley, during the trip to Auburn,
could not face the prospect of leaving, or had second thoughts
about leaving remains unclear; yet, Victor is clearly de-
stroyed by the news.

Although for the next few days Victor continues to make
the rounds of dental offices in Rome and Syracuse, he thinks
about Mary; he also becomes increasingly melancholy and
suicidal. "Oh this heartache will it ever end and if it were not
for being with Mr.Smith (a stationery salesman) and stirring
round amidst the turmoil of life it seems as I should end it.
Mary Mary come to me don't leave me so lonely." Two colony
women and his father visit Victor in Utica and try to console
him; he is, at this point, inconsolable. On a brief trip to the
community he talks at the Mansion House with James
Towner, who tries to convince him that the problem lies in
the fact that he has "forsaken God." Victor's answer is, "I told
him no I had not," and Towner seems intent on finding Victor
at fault, even suggesting that he might be crazy.

Victor's "craziness" is real enough since he has been separated from Mary, and her own response to the situation is
equally tortured. Fanny Leonard, a longtime Perfectionist
and colony member, writes in a letter to Edwin Nash about
her:

> Mary Jones has been in a good deal of tribulation this
> week having received a letter from Victor which put her
> into great distress. Of course she has been more or less in

my room, but she begins to be more cheerful now. I showed her your note that you wrote for her a few weeks since. She took it to her room to read and has never said anything to me about it since - then- now I have to stop another letter from Victor. Mrs.Towner and I have just met with Mary to talk with her about it. She takes his leaving the community and everything connected with it very hard. Does not sufficiently separate herself from him in spirit, to get relief, and consequently suffers a great deal. I do hope that she may be governed by her love for truth.

Letters to Mary are being intercepted, read, and held, and her true emotional state is unknown to Victor. He is in a state of psychic collapse and is feeling that he has been abandoned by the only true community he has ever known and by the only woman he can ever love. His pain and suffering are enormous, and they are alleviated only by his daily routine (selling stationery) and by his diary keeping. He notes one day that "I only sold 1 package this forenoon & 7 this afternoon" and is then immediately turned away from that mundane fact to deeper thoughts and emotions. "Oh how is it with Mary who has forsaken me. . . . Mary Mary come to me don't leave me so lonely." Isolation from her is softened by visits from his father, though one such encounter reduces him to tears. Without news from her and unsure about his own future, Victor leans heavily on the diary for comfort; it becomes his companion, his society, his confidant, to repeat Amiel.

When he does hear from Oneida, the news is bad. "I go to the Post Office often but no letter till tonight one from Mr. Towner saying that Mary will not see me & that all communication must be to him." Protecting her from Victor's influence is an important part of the community's scheme to save her for the society. Victor Hawley has been cast off as a bad influence, and he feels the separation deeply. "Would to God this life was ended. I walk my room till my heart is gone & I am in convulsions Mary Mary Mary would you had killed me rather than cause me suffering." Remaining unaware that Mary's own turmoil is as great as his, Victor takes the August letter as the final word and talks about "going East." Fortunately, he secures a job in a machine shop at Canastota at that time.

Despite his desire to bury thoughts of her, she remains a strong presence in his mind. The sight of some small children at his Syracuse boardinghouse makes his "heart ache more for the want of one."

During this period Victor vacillates between fantasy and melancholia. He writes to the secretary of the Woodward Expedition, asking if he could participate in their round-the-world expedition. Contrasted with this grandiose idea of world exploration is his cozy and domestic wish that he and Mary live in a little cottage together. Here, Victor's dreams become more vivid once again, and Mary plays a major role in shaping that dreamlife. "Then I dreamed that Mary or someone was with me going down stairs she had hold of my hand." Such dreams seem to comfort him and allay his worst fears. Freud's *Dream as Wish Fulfillment* is the best guide to understanding Victor's state at this time. On September 8 he dreams the perfect wish fulfillment: "I dreamed that Mary was with me & said she had not given up hope of having a child by me." His dreams bring him the assurance that the mail fails to bring, particularly after he is turned down by the Woodward Expedition. Now, Victor begins to muse about other possibilities for escape; however, these are fantasy options, such as going to the "oil fields" because wages are so low in the area, or "going South." More realistically, he considers attending a dental college. But these are mere expressions of a desire to rid himself of the burdens that are attached to his present situation. "Would to God I were on the ocean or in the other world. Here I am so lonely with an aching heart." His heart continues to ache, and in spite of the respite his dreams give him, Victor's waking hours are filled with reminders of Mary's presence and the life they have lost. At the sight of a baby he breaks into tears, and after hearing a church hymn, Victor underlines "Oh how my heart bleeds" in his diary.

For the next several weeks Mary disappears from the diary. Notices about his time at the machine shop or about his amusements ("went to see the Onandiga club play cricket") fill Victor's pages. Occasionally, he thinks of Mary within a specific context, and sometimes that memory is strong enough to force him to note it, such as when he attends the Oneida

Fair and recalls that they had gone to it on an earlier occasion. For the most part Mary recedes from the diary, and
unfortunately, it is livened only when he has to record additional rejections, such as the one from the New York College
of Dentistry ("no chance for me there").

With no chance of permanent employment and no new career possibilities on the horizon, Victor decides to return to
the colony. After making the decision, he imagines that Mary
will be thrilled by the news that he is returning; however, the
colony keeps him waiting for two weeks before letting him
know (he had sent word via Homer Barron) that he can return. When he arrives at Oneida, he learns that Mary has left
the colony and is at her brother's home in Baldwinsville!
Quickly, he makes arrangements to see her, and they are reunited on October 29 "I was with her most of the day. I asked
her if she would live with me she did not say she would.
Happy was the meeting. Oh it has brought joy to my heart.
such a happy day." It does not take her long to decide, and she
gives him the answer the very next day. She will marry him.
When he suggests that they might live at Oneida, "she turned
pale and almost fainted." Why he suggested that they live at
Oneida is unclear. Possibly, he was unaware that she had actually left the colony, or he failed to be able to conceive (after
his own period of casual labor and limited options) of a life
outside the society. Mary Jones said that "she could not go
back into the suffering she had been in. I told her she need
not. I would stand by her." Having made the great leap, they
must now face the colony once again. Victor returns the next
day and meets with Theodore Noyes. The soon-to-be-deposed
leader suggests that the best thing for them is to get married;
James Towner is much harsher in his criticism and reduces
Victor to tears.

Practical concerns now occupy him as he sets out to find
permanent work in Canastota, Syracuse, or Baldwinsville. Finally, he is able to take a job at Rome working on dental
plates for a dollar a day. On Monday, November 26 his diary
entry comes from Rome. "Mary and I have been looking for
rooms this afternoon." They go from communal life to family
life and apartment hunting. They price furniture; look at

blankets, sheeting, and bed spreads; and attend to domestic chores once they have found an apartment. Mary does return to the colony for a brief visit to pick up personal items. As the cold weather sets in, Victor's entries become briefer and briefer. As their world becomes richer and as the emotional disturbances of the previous year pass, his entries are less anxious, less weighted with trouble.

Yet, his increasingly spare entries do carry enormous emotional significance when one considers what their life at Oneida had been like and what they now had to face in the world. The community had provided everything in the way of physical necessities and group support; it was both family and friend. What it could not provide—particularly for Victor Hawley—was the special love that he needed. "Sunday December 16 1877 We finished cleaning the bedroom today with the exception of the window; Monday December 17 1877 Mary has been washing today. We put down the bedroom carpet tonight got to bed at 12:45; Tuesday December 18 1877 I put out the clothes line this morning & Mary hung out the clothes and finished washing."

And then the diary ends with one final entry. "Dec Wednesday 19 1877 Tried this morn for baby & this eve. Mary has been ironing today"

The shift from the intense, close communal routine to the private and autonomous family patterns seems like a simple one when one looks at the diary. Yet the psychological distance Victor and Mary both had traveled during the previous two years had been great. Rome was barely twenty miles from Oneida; they had come a distance that seemed greater. In this most personal of journeys they had left one country for another and traded one set of values and morals for another, becoming citizens of another nation in the process. They cleaned a cupboard for dishes, their own dishes; they bought a washtub, to perform work they must now do for themselves; they put down a bedroom carpet in a room they did not have to vacate after having sexual relations; they "tried for baby" in the morning and the evening—not under watchful eyes, as at Oneida—and whenever the urge came to them.

It would be their baby and not a community child. Mary

would have to iron every day, cook meals, and try to save money despite Victor Hawley's erratic career. Oneida had become too secure, and there were too few risks taken despite the glowing rhetoric that surrounded the stirpiculture plan, with its emphasis on scientific engineering. Victor Hawley and Mary Jones—quite ordinary people—had, by their disobedience, charted a course for themselves that was risky. They had repudiated Oneida when they made "special love," and when they took that step, they took possession of a new realm. Their world was now one of private passion, of erotic possibilities, and of private needs that had never been fully satisfied. In exchange for her baby and Victor Hawley, Mary Jones had to give up the comforts of Oneida; she had to wash clothes and take on a domestic routine. All that change took considerable courage.

John H. Noyes had hoped to "nail marriage to the cross" and subdue the destructive instincts that led individuals to exalt the flesh; stirpiculture had instead encouraged them to pursue a domestic economy rather that a "true family" economy; it had led them to possessiveness rather than to altruism. Hawley and Jones had abandoned the old community ideals by 1877 and taken up another set of ideals that incorporated romantic love, domestic security, and the exclusive and possessive love of one man and one woman. They sought comfort in each other and in the world.

The Diary of Victor Hawley
June 24, 1877–December 19, 1877

Sunday June 24 1877
I spoke to Theodore about Marys adopt ing a baby. He said he would see his Father about it. GEC asked Mary how she did she said real smart I am ready to get up & try it over again.

Monday June 25 1877
Dr Carpenter was in to see Mary this forenoon. He said she would not reach the turn of life till 43 years old, have an examination & be treated

Saturday June 30 1877

A letter was read in meeting from Dr Carpenter & one from Mr Noyes that said Mary ought not to have a baby.

Sunday July 1 1877

Mr Towner & Mrs Leonard told Mary & I that it was decided in meeting that Mary could not have another child.

Tuesday July 10 1877

I took Mary to ride to the Hamilton place. Mrs Leonard wanted Mary to use the breast pump. Mary had tried & could not. Afterwards Mrs Loveland had some words with her about it. Mrs Leonard & Mr Towner talked with me about her & wanted me to separate from her. I talked with Mary she said she did not lock Mrs Loveland & Lilly out or clench her fist at Geo E.C. She talked with Mr Towner & told him she was ready to leave the Community. So I am with her

Wednesday July 11 1877

I told Mr Towner & Mrs Leonard this afternoon that I wanted to go away with Mary if we could not have a child here as it was decided in meeting. Cornelius took Mary to the Castle & back she was very pale when she got back, it was to long a ride

Thursday July 12 1877

Mary has been abed nearly all day she cant hardly raise her head it aches and makes her feel disy to move.

Friday July 13 1877

Martha said Mr Towner was going to write to Father to day about my wanting to go away. I told Mary & Martha talked with us both & Mary promised to go with me.

Saturday July 14 1877

Mary does not feel as well to day, she did not get up till 2 P.M.

Sunday July 15 1877
I took M to the Hamilton place to ride she went to meeting to night. She helped me pull off the tow from my silk cocoons in the after noon. I carried Mary down cellar & she went to the store room to be weighed. Weight 92 3/4 lbs. I weigh 135 1/4lbs. Constance sleeps in Marys room to night. Mary feels better to night & her food has tasted good to day

Monday July 16 1877
Mary moved in Ella's room so that Mary Boles could go into the Nursery Room where she has, been. Mary was quite smart & I helped her move. I took a T Bath & then went by her door at 11 P.M. she had been asleep & awoke by the spirits. I slept with her till 2 then Mrs Loveland drew her breast & slept the rest of the night with her.

Tuesday July 17 1877
I went out over to Mud Creek hill with Mary this after noon. She does not feel quite so smart after moving but is better to night. I sleep in Mrs Loveland's room to night in the Tontine for John Leonard has painted the N. Tower windows.

Wednesday July 18 1877
Mr Towner came to the D. Office & told me that they wanted me to separate from Mary said they could get along better with out me in taking care of Mary, & said folks came to him & said that I was more of a hinderance than a help to her recov ery, & asked if I was of the same mind in regard to going away. I told him I was. He did not want me to report the talk but simply mention the separation I was with her during meeting she said she would go with me and would be well enough in about a week. I could not eat after breakfast that day.

Thursday July 19 1877
Oh how my heart aches from the separation. I only saw her a few minutes after meet ing but not to speak to her. Mr Towner was talking with Ann then with Emma He said Mary was ex cited.

Friday July 20 1877

Mr. Towner told me that Mary wanted to see me at 1 P.M. she said she was going to Auburn with Emma tomorrow. Oh that I was going instead of Emma. I could not keep from crying. Roswell got my bag for Emma. I went most to the Castle during meeting on the R. Road. After getting back about 9.45 I droped on to the bead & a feeling came over me that she would go with me. I could not eat any thing after break fast the rest of the day.

Saturday July 21 1877

Mary & Emma left in a carriage at 10.35 I watched them go from the Tower window & saw them go by the Mathewson place about 10.48. Do you love the Community better than me. I could not work at the Dentist Office I felt so. Towards evening I filed & polished some parts of my Telegraph Key to take up my attention but Oh the hours go slowly & wearily by Tis the third time she has gone from me thus & left me to stand the storm alone.

Sunday July 22 1877

At work on my Telegraph Key & Soun der all day got it pol ished & varnished & all together to night. After Herbert came up to go to bed he asked Roswell if he was going to see Aunt Marys baby R. said he guessed so. After meet ing I went most to the Cheese Factory walking back & forth till 1 P.M. & last night I only slept 4 hours I had my head out on the stone window sill for an hour or two to cool my burning brain & I only got 4 hours sleep

Monday July 23 1877

To night walked on the rail road till late but did not have my mouth organ with me which I had last night. Come back to day my Mary dear & take me of tomorrow, to lead a happy life free from this place of sorrow. In a cottage dear without these tears, a happy life we'll lead tomorrow.

Fixing Polyphemus worm box with C.A.Burt.

Tuesday July 24 1877
9 Fillings
I worked 9 ½h in the D.O. on Lily & Mary Baker & am tired to night but took my walk on the R.R. beyond the two first rams. It was a bright moon light night & I heard a red squirrel chittering & scolding away as though some thing was after it. When I got home Roswell was writing to Emma he said Mary & Emma went to Baldwinsville. Oh that I was there with Mary instead of here with a lonely aching heart.

DO9 ½h

Wednesday July 25 1877
I put in 4 gold fillings for Lily Hobart. Phoebe has the colic & I gave her some brandy during meeting. After meeting I went to Oneida & saw the Loco motives which were shoving the freight cars on to the side track out towards Canastota & 6 Locomotives started for Albany for safety from the strikers at Syracuse. It was a fine moonlight night & how I did want to go to Baldwinsville. Got to bed at 1.15.

DO9 ¼h
Thursday July 26 1877
It has been a buisy day & I am tired but for all that I take my walk on the RR after meeting. G.E.C. asked me if I gave Phoebe any thing I told him I did, he said what, I said about ⅓ glass of brandy. I had asked him if he had seen her he said no, I told him she was having a hard time of it he said that he guess ed the women were looking out for her that was said 2 hours before I gave her the brandy & he had not seen her then.

Friday July 27 1877
At 3.15 I went up stairs with Cornelius he is stuffing a Bald Eagle. I put some camphor into my cases, found para sites 3 boxes, there were 44 worms in one box which I killed. It is so dark & mudy that I have not taken my walk to night. Wearily the hours rool on waiting for thy re turn, a week has gone by since a word has passed between us.

Saturday July 28 1877
Too rainy for the walk.
Took 3 boxes & some drying boards into the T. Bath
Room. to day the specimens

Sunday July 29 1877
A lonely day.
I went up the gulf after insects I was out in a heavy rain
& got well soaked

Monday July 30 1877
Filling 2 U 2 B. for Martha
A committee of E.H.H. S.K.D. L.F.D. G.E.C. Mr. Towner,
Mrs Loveland, in the South Sitting Room for my benafit.
G.E.C. said I had done rong in giv ing Phoebe the brandy that
Theodore said I ought not to stay in the D.O. Then Mr Towner
stated how I stood. E.H.H. said the Communi ty had had forbearance long enough. Mr Towner came to me after meet ing
& said they had taken me out of the D.O. No other work was
given me. I told him that I might as well go now as to put it
off any longer and that I wanted to go & see Mary he said he
told them I would go to see her when they decided to take me
out of the D.O. He said I was at liberty to do as I was a mind
to. Evidently the whole move & purport of the meeting was to
have us go.

Tuesday July 31 1877
Mr Towner said I had better see Mary some where this
side of Auburn & as I was going off with Cornelius   Theodore
said he wanted me to go to Mr Towner & have a final setle-
ment. I did so and have been geting things ready to pack.
Myron & others have talked to me to get me to not go. Oh
when shall I have peace. They have Telagraph ed for Father.
Fredric hoped I would be prospered.

Wednesday August 1 1877
I have been getting things together to day to leave. got
my trunk packed by night. Father came about noon. Roswell
talked to me so at 6 A M that I could not go to breakfast I eat

it in Martha's Room She got it, she & Roswell picked me some
raspberries. Roswell has helped me & so has Martha & done
lots of things for me he has given me some gloves.

Thursday August 2 1877
$4.50 at Talbot House
R Finished packing my bag and off for Syracuse at 8.30
The parting was severe for a little while. At Talbot house
looked for work some & went to see if Mary was on the noon
train. Wrote to her after dinner & then looked for Dentist
work I have not made out to get any yet Out till 8 oclock.
Only 2 D.O. left to go to. Shall I try Engineering. Going to bed
10.45

Friday August 3 1877
At work for Barnes mending a plate. 1.50 then went to Dr
Cherrys to work and tried to see a couple Dentists but they
had gone from their offices. Then called on Ingersole who is a
Dentist but was half drunk & the rest gass blown over. As I
went out into the St another Dr. said it is not all gold that is
brass, good advice against the humbug.

Saturday August 4 1877
Fire Alarm 10.15
I received a letter from F Norton.
At work for Mr Cherry making a new plate. & mending a
broken one 2.00 at 3.10 P.M. I went to see 2 Dentists but could
not get work, then I went to the Salt Works which was quite a
sight seeing them boil at a rate of 100 barrels a day with a
20h. boiler & engine to blow the fire I was too late for the 8 PM
Auburn train. I have run arround so much that I am sleepy 10

Sunday August 5 1877
Up at 5 & started for Auburn 5.45. Examined directory for
the Jones boys then looked for L A Barber a dentist, then
went to Mor gan's took breakfast & then we went through a
part of the city saw Osborns place & Sewards. We went to
church then went to Will iams then to Morgans to dinner after it William came & we went to the Fork Factory then to

Williiams & his wife went to the deapot, I kept on & went to
O.C. & Saw Martha then Mary & told her I had been 72 miles
to see her. I saw Father & Ros well. I was with Mary about 2
hours ¾ with the others then Roswell took me to the deapot & I
was off for Syracuse at 2.45 at Talbot House at 4 & went to bed.

Martha got me some lunch at O.C. I was so weary that I
slept some on the cars but not much after I got here. A note
was on my plate from John Norton   I saw him a little while. I
have been making gas for Mr Cherry this afternoon.

Tuesday August 7 1877

I played on my mouthoran in the evening I wrote a letter
to Mary last evening. I told her that I went 86 miles before I
saw her & about 120 miles in all most of them to see her.
Making a plate & Fixing tools & a treadle to a grind stone
lathe in Dr. Cherries Office. At supper I felt as though Mary
had got my letter sent this morning & had made up her mind
to come with me.

Wednesday August 8 1877

A letter from Mr Towner Criticising my course in send
ing Martha to Mary without letting her go to some one else
first.

Alfred called on me and said I would soon forget all this I
said so you think   It seemed as though my heart would break
he talked to me so. I wrote to Mr Towner to night asking his
pardon Alfred took my watch watch to Chapins.

Thursday August 9 1877

At C E Cherry's fixing tools. 65 C B Marks called in in the
afternoon & said all was quiet at O.C. A letter from F.N. After 7 P.M. I walked up Fayette St by the Orphan Asylum and
back via Genesee St. Oh Mary Mary why don't you answer
my letter. I feel lonly to night without you Come to me my
Dearest love.

Friday August 18 1877

GD Allen called at Cherry's Office & gave me my night
shirt that I left in Marthas Room. No work from Mr Cherry to

day I went & saw Mr Nellis but he had none. After dinner I went to Ingersons & we went to a broker & bought some tools for 10.00 which were some rusty but were rusty. I worked some of them over & pollished & scraped the ivory handles.

Saturday August 11 1877

Finished fixing tools & bought $26.00 worth of Dentists mat erial and started out & went up East Genesee St to 215 the on to Fayette St to 28 Beach St & back I only got .15cts for treating a tooth. Some of my clothes were moved from Room 36 to 42 when I did not know it & I began to think they were stolen.

Sunday August 12 1877

A lonesom forenoon I went to the Central Baptist Church & heard Mr Hollenbeck Preach then went to the park & sat for an hour lone ly enough, wanting to see Mary. At dinner at 1 Mr C L Smith with whom I had previously spoken to asked me to his room & I did $1.50 worth of work filling teeth for him. I think it came in answer to prayer & the blessing that the minister asked God to give us. Thank God.

(7)*

Monday August 13 1877

I have been running arround Syracuse selling Stationary for Mr C L Smith I sold seven packages. I have been packing to leave for the East in the morning.

10

Tuesday August 14 1877

Globe Hotel Oneida

I went to Canastota and Mr Smith came on the next train I sold 7 pacages and we left for Oneida at 1.22 where I sold 3 more.

I got a letter from Mary in which she says she will stay in the Community & will not go with me. Oh God why am I thus

---

*This leading number and similar numbers in subsequent entries refer to the number of packages sold and not to hours worked.

forsaken it is a bitter day to me My heart bleeds & tears rool
down my face to the pages I write to her at Oneida

9–1
Wednesday August 15 1877
Rome
There is music in the Willet house this eve. I sold 3 packages this A.M. & got my watch & we left for Rome 1.30 P.M. I
sold 6–1 packages this P.M. My heart sank with in me this
forenoon 2 or 3 times as I felt that Mary had got my letter. Oh
this heart ache will it ever end if it was not for being with Mr
Smith and stirring around amidst the turmoil of life here it
seems as though I should end it.

8.
Thursday August 16 1877
Rome
I only sold 1 package this forenoon & 7 this afternoon they
went better I am tired to night. Oh how is it with Mary who
has forsaken me would to God she would come to me. Life
would be dreary enough if it was not for Mr C.L.Smith's jovial
conversation which helps to keep my spirits up. Mary Mary
come to me don't leave me so lonely.

(8)
Friday August 17 1877
Utica
Father was on the train when we were on the way from
Rome. I was intending to stop at Whitesborough but kept on
to Utica & was with him Mrs Story & Mrs Hawley till they
left here at 11'30 A.M. I cried when I was with him most of the
time in Bags Hotel after that I went nearly half way to
Whitesborough selling packages. I went into the cotton mills
in Utica. I saw Dr Cook.

(21)
Saturday August 18 1877
Utica
14 packages in the forenoon & 7 in the after noon. I wrote

to Mary & sent it to her by last nights mail   I wrote to her come here to see me before I leave Monday morn ing.

Sunday August 19 1877

C L Smith & I went down & took a swim in the Mohawk river after breakfast. About noon I called on Dr Hitchcock but could not get work of him, and then I called on Dr Matt Cook. About 4 took Mr Smith up & we saw the Pigieons & his insects after super I told him I was looking for work.

(30)
Utica Made 2.10
Monday August 20 1877

I have not eaten any supper I sold 9 in the forenoon & when I came to the Mansion House they said Mr Towner was looking for me. He came in about 12 & talked with me He tried to have me say that I had forsaken God I told him *no* I had not and it seemed as though he wanted to make out that I was crazy or something of the sort My God why is it Do help Oh Lord. Mr S was too late for the train so I took 59 pkg's & sold 10 up St & went to York Mills & sold 11. I am to wait here 2 or 3 days to see Mary.

30–1–7cts Made 1.78
Tuesday August 21 1877

I sold 7 in the forenoon & 12 in the after noon. Oh why dont Mary come here I am all alone I was sick with a head ache this morn ing. Not a word do I get from Mr Towner & here I am waiting in suspence my heart is *acheing, acheing.* I love God as much as ever and through all trial I shall cling to him, but it seems as though life would be short if this lasts much longer. Mary Mary do come to me my heart is break ing.

9 Utica
Wednesday August 22 1877

I can hardly work I feel so. I go to the Post Office often but no letter till to night one from Mr Towner saying Mary will not see me & that all communication must be to him. Would

to God this life was ended. I walk my room till my heart is
gone & I am in convulsions Mary Mary Mary would you had
killed me rather than cause this suffering.

6 Utica &c
Thursday August 23 1877
I lay down in the night by the window with my pants for a
pillow & droped to sleep for a short time after walking the
room. I awoke at 2 & went to bed but did not sleep any more.
It has been a hard day I walked to Washington Mills & took
the cars to Clayville & back to Utica I sold 6 packages & gave
1 for my dinner The clerk of Mr Priest advised me to go back
near my friends for work.

Utica Syracuse & Canastota
Friday August 24 1877
I went Canastota & found that I still had a chance to work
in the Knife Works at 1.50 a day so I went to Syracuse & got
my trunk & came back. I saw Mr Burnham & told him that I
was going East. I got a place to board at Mr Madison Reynolds for 3.50 per week. I wrote a letter to C.L.Smith & sent it
to Albany & a postal to Utica Post Office & one to Mr Towner.
I was weary of the turmoil of the city & did not stop there
long.

Canastota
Saturday August 25 1877
At work in the Knife Works turning mandrils for emery
wheels & drilling dies. It has been a lonesom day & there was
one spell it seemed as though I should drop to the floor & my
right was numb. Mary Mary you have caused this Oh why
dont you come to me you feel it deeply I know espec ially to
day during the rain. I am tired to night. Oh God help me help
me.

Sunday August 26 1877
I have been in the house most all day I lay down for some
time after breakfast & walked out a little ways before dinner
or rather supper at 3 P.M. after that I read a while & played

on my mouth organ in the evening. My heart aches for thee. There are 3 Children 2 girls & 1 boy which help some to pass the hours although it makes my heart ache more for the want of one.

Monday August 27 1877
The day has been a long one & my thoughts are of thee Why Oh Why dont you come to me & make my life happier in this dreary world.

Tuesday August 28 1877
C R Marks & C M Leonard came to the Knife fac tory this afternoon I saw them just as I was going down stairs. I asked Charles to see Mr Towner or Alfred about getting me some Machine tools and a box to keep them in. Oh that it had been Mary that came with Charles instead of Charlotte.

Wednesday August 29 1877
I carry my dinner to the shop now days as Mrs M Reynolds & assistant go hop picking during the day. Taking my dinner saves me a long hasty walk at noon as we have only 50 minutes nooning & quit at 5 Saturdays.

Thursday August 30 1877
I have been making emery wheel man drils when not drilling dies or other job work. Case hardened the mandrils to day Mr S More talked with me about the work in the shop and said that after Christmas they would only run 8 hours so that makes rather short wages for me

Friday August 31 1877
Finished boring out the driving pulleys for 15 mandrils. Repaired a drilling machine & fixing a grindstone arbor. It has been a sorrowful day to me. When making a reamer at the anvil it flew from the tongs and hit my nose & just above my left eye. it made my nose bleed for some time but I was thankful that it did not hit my eye.

Saturday September 1 1877
Turning the bearings to a grind stone shaft and shrinking
on some colars to make them larger, then worked on a belt
tightener.
In the evening I wrote to F Norton.

Sunday September 2 1877
I have been writing to Mr D Macauley of Indianapolis,
Ind. Secretary of the Wood ruff Expedition around the world
to see if I could get a chance to go. This afternoon I fixed a
music box instrument that was in an album for Mrs Reynolds
in the evening. I gave the family some peaches.

Monday September 3 1877
My letters were put into the Post Office this noon it has
been a long dreary day wet & rainy. Carmie Min nie & Florence sang in the evening which helped to pass the time But
Oh if Mary was here she would help to pass the time far
pleasant er. I went to bed at 9 this eve and slept a few minutes then awoke & could not get to sleep till past 12.

Tuesday September 4 1877
Turning driving pulleys on emery wheel shafts this P.M.
pined them on in the forenoon.
In the evening practiced on John M flute and My mouth
organ the folks have all gone to bed at 9 P.M. for Mr B. gets up
about five to start the fire & Mrs Reynolds & Julia get up
about 5.30. John & I get up at 5.50 & the children at 6.30

Wednesday September 5 1877
Threading nuts for the mandrils it takes about ¾ of an
hour to each one as there is no tap & the thread has to be cut
in a lathe including the boring and facing. Some of the shop
boys are geting ready for a game of cricket ball with the Chitenango boys tomorrow. I did not drink any tea for din ner or
supper & went to bed 9.15 & went to sleep. I awoke soon after
10. & lay awake till past 12. then I dreamed that Mary or
some one was with me going down stairs she had hold of my
hand &

Thursday September 6 1877

Making a drill to bore the emery wheel woods & commenced boring them in the forenoon in the after noon nailing on laging to some pulleys on the line shaft. The shop boys are most all gone to the cricket match. After quit ing I asked Mr More if he could give me 1.50 per day through the winter as they are only going to run 8 hours he said he would see about it

Friday September 7 1877

Finished boring the wheels & turned three   It has been a long sober day. One time I looked up & the Office boy was watching & I was so sober. Oh little does he know how my heart aches & I had to turn away for the tears came in spite of every thing & my head aches I feel so. In the eve Mrs Farrar came in & talked gayly for a little while, but I wish it was Mary that came. I finished turning & now they are ready for the leathers.

Saturday September 8 1877

Saturday night 8th I dreamed that Mary was with me & she said she had not given up the hope of having a child by me.

Sunday September 9 1877

I went to the Post Office 3 times to day & finely got a Postal & paphlet from the Woodruff expedition around the world   No chance for me to go. A walk after dinner of chicken when going saw some one with a baby I could not help crying. In church in the evening they sang The gates left ajar for me, then Im going home, & Only waiting, tears would fill would fill my eyes. *Oh how my heart bleeds.*

Monday September 10 1877

At Work on a couple large emery wheels Shall I go to a Dental College or South or to the Oil region for wages are too low here. Would to God I were on the ocean or in the other world. Here I am so lonely with an aching heart.

It seems as though Mary had a chill last night or within a few nights Helping put on leathers

Thursday September 11 1877
Fixing tools, puting on leathers & cutting off 6 irons for emery wheels. After super Florenc Reynolds & I went to Mrs Farr after some butter. I thought what shall I work for now that Mary has forsaken me shall I get a lot of Entomological books or turn Dentist.

Wednesday September 12 1877
Turning 6 emery wheel shafts. & sweeping Mr Newhouse came into the shop to day and asked how long I had been there & what I was getting for wages, he did not know before that I was at work there. I got a letter from F Norton & answered it to night Wrote one to Morgan Jones & one to C L Smith. It is 12 oclock & I must go to bed. my head has felt bad all day inclined to the catarrh from mental strain.

Thursday September 13 1877
Fitting on colars & thredding &c.
Tears fill my eyes as the hours go slowly by

Friday September 14 1877
The 6 shafts are ready for case hard ening the ends At dinner Mrs Reynolds said that I was going to have company as the tea gave me too
Mr & Mrs Reynolds & Julia Carman went to a wedding this afternoon. Oh where is mine

Saturday September 15 1877
Making pulleys for two large emery wheels

Sunday September 16 1877
Went to the Methodist Church with Mr Reynolds It was the minis ters last sermon. I took a key to Mrs Ransom and spent the evening there Mr Ransom, Mead Barnet & his brother were there. Mrs & Mr Reynolds & Julia Carmen Carmen came over also & spent the evening there.

Monday September 17 1877
Making pulleys &c

Tuesday September 18 1877
I helped John Ryan move up his truck to Mr Lansings where John's is going to board himself.

Wednesday September 19 1877
Helping William Lindley make a machine to bend some strap irons on for wagons

Thursday September 20 1877
Finished the mac hine at 10 then we worked the rest of the day bending irons my head ached & I had to quit a few minutes before the quiting time it was hot and hard work & a trip hammer near by made so much noise that the last hour it seemed as though it was pounding my head. I vomited when I got home & only took a cup of tea for supper.

Friday September 21 1877
Finished bending the irons at 10 then went to sawing off plank for the wagon woods

Work ½ day
Saturday September 22 1877
Commenced sliting the plank, then sawing ebony & lig-numvita for knife handles. Shop closed at noon & in the after noon I went to see the Onandaga club play cricket with the Canastota club The Onandaga boys were from Syracuse & won by 8 wickets. In the evening heard the brass band play at the opening of the Two good House.

Sunday September 23 1877
I called John Ryan after break fast. Sent a letter to F Norton yesterday.

Monday September 24 1877
Slitting Wagon woods

Tuesday September 25 1877
Planing Wagon woods. I thought this afternoon that if I could see Green Smith perhaps he would pay my pass age on the Woodruff expedition if I would get him a lot of birds.

Wednesday September 26 1877
Planing Wagon woods

Thursday September 27 1877
Sawing & boring the ends of the W woods. It is Fair day
at Oneida & tears run down my face as I thought of Mary &
the ride we took to see the balloon go up years ago. I saw the
balloon at 4.10 P.M.

John Ryan has come back to Mr Reynolds. John & I called
on Mr Lans ing to night. He said his son would be back from
London the 20 of next month.

Friday September 28 1877
Trimming & smooth the ends and turning two lignumvita
steps for water wheels.

Saturday September 29 1877
Painting the woods & turning two more water wheel steps

Sunday September 30 1877
A lonesom day I went to Mr Lansings after dinner and
looked at his books. There was one containing the description
& illus tration of beetles & birds found during the Pacific R R
Survey.

Worked ½ day
Monday October 1 1877
Grinding iron hand le knives in the forenoon.

I was told that there was no work for the rest of the day,
so I went to Syracuse saw Cherry, Ingerson Matson, & Mr
Barnes he sketched off a letter for me to send to Dental Coleges. I wrote off one to send to New York D.C. when I got
back after eat ing supper which was on the table.

46.50
Tuesday October 2 1877
Mead Barnet shot a squirel yes tuerday with a rifle and
another to day. After writing a letter to Philadelphia Dental
College & calling on Mr More I went through the Cemetery to
the woods to shoot squirrels got one red one & a chipmuck

½ day for Mr Madison
Wednesday October 3 1877
About noon Mr Madison gave me a job threading a nut &
a screw to fit it, 4 to the inch

6 ¾h Mr M $3.60
Thursday October 4 1877
Finished them about 10 then did some turning for him
which took till 2.45 He gave me $3.60 I shall have to pay for
the use of the lathe.

October Friday 5 1877
In the shop a while then at Mr Lansings Reading
Got a letter from New York College of Dentistry no
chance for me there.

Saturday October 6 1877
In the shop seeing them make the different parts of the
knives & fixing my mercury bottle

Sunday October 7 1877
Spent the day at Mr Lansings look ing over his books &
reading
I went to Church in evening & to a temperance lecture

Monday October 8 1877
Packing my truck & waiting for letter from Phil adelphia
& F Norton

Canastota Tuesday October 9 1877
Letter from Pha. to day. I called on Mr Smith Dentist &
whilst there about 11.30 I saw Otis, Gorge Kellogg & James
Hatch go by with the black team.
I went down by the factory but think they did not stop as I
saw no more of them. I sawed some wood in the afternoon &
made a little candy in the evening for the children as the
folks have gone to a temperance lecture

Syracuse
Wednesday October 10 1877
I went to Syracuse. Called on Drs. Cherry, Nellis, & Barnes, No chance to work at dentistry then I went to see if I could get some work in any confectionary shops or manufactories did make out to day shall try again in the morning.

Syracuse
Thursday October 11 1877
When going back from the Eastern part of Syracuse I jumped on to the train. Mrs Robinson & Mr Van Velzer were on the train he beckon ed to me. They said Mary was at O.C. Phoebe is better so as to be out some. Johnston's Agent said Tremain at Rome wanted help. No work in Syracuse. When going back to Canastota I saw Homer Barron on the train and told him to tell Mr Towner that I wanted to go back to the Community and that I would stop in Canastota a day or two to see him.\

Canastota
Friday October 12 1877
A rainy day and it is lonely wait ing here with nothing to do but cut a little wood for Mr Reynolds. I go to the P.O. but nothing there. A thrill passed through me last night when I new Mary heard that I wanted to come back to the Community. No one from O.C. and nothing at the P. Office for me.

Canastota
Sunday October 14 1877
I went off with Mr Hernshaw and an other man to shoot wood cock. They had two dogs. I was with them two hours and they shot three wood cock.
Oh why this waiting and not a word from O.C.
I went to a temper ance meeting in the evening.

Rome
Monday October 15 1877
I am off for Rome in the morning bag and baggage.
Did not make out to strike a bargain with Dr L.F.Tre

main. I called on the other Dentists and at the Confectionary shops.

Dinner at the Northern Hotel .30

Board at Mrs Green's 4.00 per week or 1.20 per day 13 Dominick St.

Tuesday October 16 1877
Looking arround for work called on Dr Robberts and saw him put in a large gold filling in about ½ hour. Dr A B Cowles said perhaps he would give me some work tomorrow

Wednesday October 17 1877
At work for Dr A.B.Cowles, I finish ed a partial plate and put two more into flasks.

Thursday October 25 1877
a letter from O.C. saying that I might return

Rome
Friday October 26 1877
Mr Cows put in a Gold filling for me 2.00

Rome Syracuse Oneida
Saturday October 27 1877
Off to Syracuse and disposed of my instruments then to Oneieda When I met Martha I felt as though Mary had gone I asked Mr Towner he said yes to Baldwinsville
OC & Canastota

Sunday October 28 1877
I went to Canastota and got some letters but not a word from Mary   I walked there & back.

Baldwinsville
Monday October *29 1877*
I awoke at 12.15 and went to Oneida on to Baldwinsville and and met Mary at her brother James

I was with her most of the day. I asked her if she would live with me she did not say she would. Happy was the meeting. Oh it has brought joy to my heart such a happy happy day

Baldwinsville & O C
Tuesday October 30 1877
Mary came to me in the morning and said she would marry me I asked her if I should go to OC and to W.C. if she could go to OC and be happy she turned pale and almost fainted. She said she could not go back into the suffering she had been in. I told her she need not I would stand by her   Off to O.C. at 7

O.C. to Rome
Wednesday October 31 1877
I told Theodore why I went to see Mary at Bald winsville and he said the best thing for us to do was to get married.
Mr Towner made me cry he talked so to me
Cornelius took me to Oneida I called on Mr Smith then went to Rome. I went to Mrs Green's to sleep where I have boarded

Rome to Canastota, Syracuse & Baldwinsville
Thursday November 1 1877
I saw Mr Tremain who said he would give me $26.00 per month so I am going to work for him if I dont find a better place at better prices then off to Baldwinsville in the evening Mary & Fidelia (Jameses wife) were at the depot. Mary felt as though she would meet me and I was glad to see her.

Baldwinsville
Saturday November 3 1877
Looking for work but have not made out to get any yet

Weding eve
Tuesday November 6 1877

Baldwinsville to Auburn
Wednesday November 7 1877

Auburn
Saturday November 10 1877

Auburn
Sunday Nov 11 1877

Auburn to Rome
Monday November 12 1877
I went to the Big Wollen Mill with William Jones to see if
we could get work then to the Fifth wheel shop. William
steped under a waitor that was coming down. I said look out
& he jump ed out. No work Mary & I took the train for Syracuse at 11 in the afternoon she went to Baldwinsville & I
went to Rome in the evening

Rome looking for Rooms to Rent
Tuesday November 13 1877
    Looking for 2 rooms to rent on the ground floor, finaly
decided to try at Mr Bowen @ 1.50 per week, rooms furnished.
I shall board here till Mary comes @ 3.25 per week

Wednesday November 14 1877
    At work for Mr Tre main @ $1.00 per day or rather $26.00
per month for the winter
    I sent a letter to Mary this morning At work on plate
work.

Thursday November 15 1877
    Vulcanized a plate just before quiting Sent a letter to
Martha & one to F Norton

Friday November 16 1877
    I had to vulcanize the plate over this forenoon as it was
not hard enough. I vulcanized another after supper to night
got through at 9.20

Wednesday November 21 1877
A letter this noon from Mary

Rome

Friday November 23 1877

Mary came this noon & walked up to Mr Tremains Office. I had been to the other train to meet her & was just start ing out to go again but expected she would stop at Oneida till evening. This is a *happy* evening for me.

Monday November 26 1877

Mr Tremain & I finish ed 2 plates this forenoon. Mary & I have been looking for rooms this afternoon

Tuesday November 27 1877

F.A. Marks called to day. He went up & saw Mary first, then came to the Office with her to see me then they went & looked at the rooms we think of hiring at $4.00 per Month & a cottage 8.00 per.M.

Thursday November 29 1877

At work till 11 then prized furniture for Mary & I

Friday November 30 1877

Fixing Book Case & tools. Looking at blankets, Sheeting, spreads &c with Mary after geting through work at the D. Office

December Saturday 1 1877

Sweeping and dusting the whatnots in the afternoon prizing furniture and cooking utensils with Mary.

Wednesday December 5 1877

Mary left on the 8.48 A.M. Train for O.C. Mrs Bowen wante more than 5.00 per week for our board or that Mary should do more work so to keep the place I gave 1.00 more tonight.

A. Socialist came the P.M. about 5.00 Wrote a letter to F Norton this eve. A rainy day.

Friday December 7 1877

Mary came this evening on the 6.37 P M train. She got Husks, Tick, Sheets, Tin ware lamp Crockery &c at O.C. & Oneida

Saturday December 8 1877
Mary got 1 ton Chestnut Coal @ 4.75 We took our last
meal at Mr Bowens this morning. We went & paid Mr
Nicholson rent for a small house back off of 122 James St.
Mary got a stove & had it put up at $12.00 We had O.C. bread
& an apple for dinner no seat but board from the stove to the
scutle. I got a trunk, box, & husks fr the deapo & out trunks
from Mr Bowens @ .50 & Mary got the furniture
Husks in bed & we went to bed about 12

Sunday December 9 1877
Got our clothes from Mrs Bowen she had not ironed mine
which was provoking Washing the cupboard for dishes. After
supper looking over husks till 12.30 & got to bed about 1
oclock

Monday December 10 1877
Mary went to the deapot to get a trunk check of John Lord
but he did not come. A letter at noon from Cornelius saying
John wuld come tomorrow.

Tuesday December 11 1877
Mary got the trunk of Crockery &c from the deapot

Saturday December 15 1877
Alfred came to day and went up and saw Mary, she came
down with him in the evening we got some groceries ash sif-
ter 20c &c Washtub 1.00 2 ¼lbs boiling meat .18

Sunday December 16 1877
We finished cleaning the bed room to day with the exception of the window

Monday December 17 1877
Mary has been washing to day
We put down the bedroom carpet to night got to bed about
12.45

Tuesday December 18 1877
I put out the clothes line this morning & Mary hung out
the clothes and finished washing

Wednesday December 19 1877
Tried this morn for baby & this eve Mary has been ironing to day

Memoranda

Memoranda
Office

68.58	8.23		175 lbs
Feb 14,	$60.87	Cr 10.25	36 Flues
	7.71		16″ Diam

25th2 Night Shirts   2′ High
    10 yds @ 10 ½cts   = 1.45   3′ "with dome & Sshpd
        making   .45   Cement for

Aquarium
    4 Shirsts @ 1.20   = 4.80   Scientific A.Oct. 13
    4 Handierchiefs @ .23 = .92   1877 p.236.13
    3 Boxes Collars @ .14 = .39   +3
                         $7.71   Jas Helmer 13.00

F.Norton 392 Chapel St.
New Haven, Conn.
Room 4 Smith's Building

S.V. Andrews 36 Boerum Place
Brooklyn, N.Y.

175 lbs
36 Flues
16″ Diam
2′ High
3′ High with dome &
cement for Aquarium in
Scientific A. Oct 13 1877 p236 .13
Jas Helmer 13.00
8.00 for him

Cash Account—January

	Received	Paid
4 Oneida Tickets		
15.03 On Hand	17.37	
Clarence Dr 2.30		
Springs	.35	
	1.95	
Lock	.25	
cash	.37	
	1.33	
	1.33	
	0.00	
—Feb		
Emma Austin		.50
—March		
Dentistry		1.50
Shoes		2.25
Slips		2.25
Meat		.30
½ Bananas		.30
4 Doz Corks D		.10
Class D		.10
Beet		.05
Armlets		.25
Comb		.25
50 Oranges		.75
D.W. at Smith's		.75
—April		
On hand	9.14	
DW	4.00	
DW	5.45	
Bottle Case		1.50
Brusshes C Hair		.16
Tooth picks		.10
Corks		.10

Peanuts		.20
Pheobe Sibley		.25
—May		
2 Fares to Rome		.52
Dinner		.50
Candy		.25
L W		5
Gum		.10
Boxes		.18
Two fares to Rome & Ret		1.04
D W		2.00
2 Dinners		.50
8 Bannanas		.40
12 Oranges		.25
Toys		.38
D W	.25	
June		
2 Cocoa Nutes		.16
L W		.10
Gum		.24
Wine Cloth		1.65
Tarlatan net		1.85
D.W.	.50	
Sep.Calender		1.75
Cork & Postage		1.40
I.Pins		5.00
November		
Loging		.50
Ticket Ro-Sy		.98
D W		.75
[No date]		
Cloth Shoes		2.25
Slippers		2.25
Black Straw Hat		1.25
2 pr.of suspenders		1.00

Napkin holder	.25
Picture	.50
Mending shoes	.20
Rubbers	.65
Pictures	
5 Boxes colars @ 12	.60
Summer Suit	12.50
½ dozen Stoereno Locks	3.13
2 Neckties	.16
Mending Coat &	
pants	1.00
2 Insect cases	7.50

 CHAPTER SIX

The Future of Stirpiculture

*This one thing above all, I think you need
to learn as I am learning it—that no sound
work can be done in building communities,
without very careful selection of material—
more careful than any of us have yet been
qualified to exercise. Communism is not for
swine, but only for the sons and daughters
of God.*

—John H. Noyes,
Niagara Journal, 1881

*O*he Hawley-Jones union lasted and, contrary to the scientific prognosis at Oneida, produced five children, including a set of twins. Victor and Mary's life after Oneida cannot be told in any detail other than that they probably never returned to live there, with Victor dying in 1893 and Mary in 1906. Relatives of them both have memories of stories about Mary being "tough" and "quarrelsome," but there is no evidence of those traits or much else in the recently opened Oneida archives. All that survives of their life consists of this diary, a few letters, the scientific evidence found in the stirpiculture data, and a final, disturbing letter about Mary's last years.

Victor Hawley, according to those records, joined Oneida on September 29, 1854 and seceded on July 2, 1877, weighed 136 pounds and was 5'9" tall. Mary Jones joined April 27, 1858 and left October 25, 1877, weighed 108 pounds and stood 5'¼" tall; she was delivered of a "dead child" on June 24, 1877. Mary's name was mentioned in an 1889 letter to Alfred Hinds and Elizabeth Hawley thanking several people for a box of clothing sent to California.

Victor and Mary had left in late October 1877 and John H. Noyes had fled the community for Niagara Falls, Canada, in June 1879 never to return. Mistakenly, he had feared arrest or prosecution by local authorities, and the colony itself was fast falling apart. Ironically, Noyes, who had a Napoleonic view of himself, once joked about being sent to St. Helena with his Josephine, Harriet Holton. She did, in fact, go with him. The breakup of the community was caused by a complex of events, personalities, and issues. Noyes's age; his attempt to turn authority over to Theodore in 1877 the clash among factions within the group supporting change to a "regular" marriage and sexual relationship and those supporting either a modified form or the old order; and the stirpiculture experiment itself, unleashing passions and forces that could not be contained by new arrangements and leaders, all contributed to the breakup. When Noyes had introduced the idea of the experiment in 1868 he hoped it would radicalize the community and move it onto new ground. It was to be both a grand experiment and a catalyst for a new Oneida.

In an 1892 letter written (but never sent) to Anita New-comb McGee, the anthropologist who was studying the colony, Theodore Noyes described in a particularly lucid and dispassionate manner the heart of the complex-marriage arrangement. McGee had written earlier saying that the "monogamic instinct" was the chief factor in overthrowing the complex-marriage system, and the Hawley-Jones affair underlines that thesis. Theodore believed that his father's aging and his turning over of seignorial rights to his son and others had created a major problem. When Theodore assumed the leadership, he had malaria, was in a weakened condition, and was unable to carry out his sexual duties (in addition to being an unsuitable leader), with the result that "father was obliged to carry out the responsibility of a social center after he had begun to lose his attractiveness by age." The key issue was not simply a sexual one, but one involving primal power.

I cannot free my mind of an impression which was present all through the struggle, and without which it is difficult to account for all the facts, and the bitterness of the
contest, and that is, that the control of the young women
was pictured in the inner recesses of the minds of all persons of intelligence, as a matter not of committees and
Councils, but of individuals and men- in short a prize to be
contended for.

For Theodore and his father the power to introduce virgins into complex marriage was at the heart of the system
that kept the community in place. When that principle was
abandoned, or when it failed to work effectively, such as in
1877–1878 there was sexual anarchy, or what they called "license." In this unsent letter Theodore outlined—clearly and
for the first time—how central sexual control was to the success of the colony. Without the lord of the manor, John H.
Noyes, exercising that control there was social and sexual anarchy, just as there was in the world. Theodore's thoughts
about this continuing need for control must be quoted at
length, and Mary Jones's pregnancy should be seen within
the context of this philosophy.

The seduction of a young girl entails fearful consequences in ordinary society and, in my opinion, society does
not deal with the men concerned in such iniquities with
anything like due severity. But in our society, the consequences of the first sexual experience were to lead the
women on to an honorable position, in every respect as desirable, from our point of view, as in hers in a monogamic
marriage. Now this is the whole matter of the induction of
the young women into complex marriage was by common
consent left to father and those whom he designated. Of the
details of the practice I know very little. The rank and file of
the Community who were admitted to intimacy with the
young women, found them experienced married women; and
to have this the common state of all the attractive young
women I, and those who thought as I did, regarded as the
keystone of the social fabric. It eliminated the whole mass of
sentiment and passion which, in the world, revolves around
the question of virginity, and thus removed us so far from
the fashions of the world that we had a sentiment of honor

peculiar to ourselves which was as effective in maintaining
self respect as is the dignity of the matrons in monogamous
marriage and, as far as I know, this condition was aspired to
as much in the married condition in ordinary society.

As to father's practice in this function of first husband, I
have always been satisfied with his announced rule-that as
soon as the growing boy or girl arrived at a state of development such that they should be led into safe, improving relations to forestall unsafe, dangerous ones. If it be admitted
that our state as a whole was desirable, then the sooner a
girl was launched upon it after she arrived at the requisite
control for insuring moderation. Moderate association with
men is normal to any healthy women beyond the age of pu-
berty, and she is better for it in every way, if social conditions are honorable and attractive.

After developing his rationale for the exercise of sexual
seignorial rights—placing it on both chivalric and practical
grounds—he then turned to a key factor in his father's sexual
and social power.

In a society like a community, the young and attractive
women form the focus toward which all social rays converge;
and the arbiter to be truly one, must possess the confidence
and to a certain extent exercise his power by genuine sexual
attraction to a large extent. To quite a late period father
filled this situation perfectly. He was a man of quite extraordinary attractiveness to women, and he dominated
them by his intellectual power and social "magnetism"
super-added to intense religious convictions to which young
women are very susceptible. The circle of young women he
trained when he was between 40 and 50 years of age, were
by a large majority his devoted friends throughout the trouble which led to dissolution.

"Father" Noyes, as he was known in the community, was
the force that kept the competition for the virgins at bay, the
sexual instructor of the young, and the one who could (in the
end) make decisions about the sexual life of the colony. When
he delegated that authority to a committee, or when he was
unable to perform the office himself, the system of organiza-

tion and control broke down. Theodore wrote that he "regarded the abolition of virginity from the social state as the keystone, and it was precisely here that complex marriage was attacked." Taking on his father's role, his power, his authority was not what Theodore wanted. They were a burden that his father had borne, and Theodore preferred the "life of a recluse." He had seen enough of his father's life to know that the cares and responsibilities outweighed any "imagined pleasures." "The power of regulating the sexual relations of the members," he wrote, was "by far the most effectual means of government."

This sexual theocracy at Oneida became unglued, I would contend, with the introduction of stirpiculture and with the unleashing of passions inherent in the Hawley-Jones affair. Mary Jones had been "started" by an unwilling man *directed by his father to do so*. Despite her pregnancy, despite the efforts to keep them apart, despite doubts and setbacks, Hawley and Jones maintained their love for one another and their desire for one another, finally going on to lead a separate life, a life of monogamous passion in a larger community.

In a paper and in a letter to Harriet Skinner in November 1879 John H. Noyes wrote to the community at Oneida about the "Future of Stirpiculture." In his retirement at Niagara Falls he continued to receive visitors, to maintain a social life (he fell in love with a young girl and later a visiting English lady), and to offer advice about the colony and its future. He was, after all, still a potent figure for all groups at the colony. By the time Noyes wrote these reflections, complex marriage had been abandoned, couples like Jones and Hawley were pairing up, and the view from inside Oneida suggested that the breakup was inevitable. Noyes was still unable, however, to give up his grand scheme though there was abundant evidence around suggesting that it had ended as a social experiment. Yet he still wanted to continue his plan of creating a "superior breed of men and women." Preliminary evidence drawn from the children born in the 1870s suggested to him that Oneida had created a "superior collection" and that these would form the nucleus of a new society "if we can keep it from being swept into the mongrelism of the world."

The end of complex marriage had—Noyes mistakenly thought—freed members from the love intrigues in the community and all the persecutions from the outside world. What he suggested was the introduction of the "circumscribed marriage." "By this I mean that we should keep the community inclosure sound, and place ourselves under not a law but a rule of persuasive grace, that as our children grow up their marriage shall be kept, so far as it lies in our power, within that inclosure." It would be comparable to what the Jewish race had always done and continued to do and to what the "whole world" is working out now. This "universal" law was already at work (the Jews being the only example he gave), and he hoped that forty families at Oneida might—instead of choosing complete communism as they had in 1848—choose one another as persons of good blood and good culture, and agree to consider themselves as an association for circumscribed marriages, pledging themselves to bring about by all honorable means the fittest possible mating of their rising generations within their own circle.

Noyes foresaw a day not so far off when there would be "as much enthusiasm for perfecting the blood of human beings as there is for starting choice breeds of horses, dogs, and strawberries . . . !" He believed that by adopting "marriage"—what he called "monogamic marriage"—he could push forward his new plan, and the Oneidans could "propogate as fast as we can." Such a plan might also be suggested to socialists as the basis for new communities "for the express purpose of thorough breeding." Better, he thought, than the present members in socialistic communities who seek "pleasant company" and an "easy way to get their bread and butter." This "breeding in and in" and these breeding colonies (with Oneida taking the lead) practicing circumscribed marriage would maintain the utopian quality of life at Oneida and help members to continue to deal with that great question with which they had always struggled: "whether amativeness can be subordinated to the public weal?" Marriage within the "home circle," as he called it, marriage within the "inclosure"—such were the terms he used to describe this new community of domestic peace, this community of superior beings, this community at the same time apart from the world and leading it into the next century. Harold Bloom, in *The American Religion: The Emergence of the Post-Christian Nation,* rightly sees that Oneida exalted the communal at the expenses of the individual. "Because the biblical dispensation was ended, the saints were to live for perfection alone, and so a purely individual relation to the Spirit now had to yield to a communal good, which alone could secure sinlessness. Possessive sexual intercourse was to be set aside for the higher good and more serene social kinship"(70).

This monastic notion of the enclosure was never adopted, even though many members remained within Oneida or settled near one another, as did the group that went to Anaheim, California. Members married outside the enclosure, allowed their passions to wander, and produced a generation of children who made the Oneida silverware plate synonymous with marriage. To the very end Noyes continued to use his barnyard metaphors but the new enclosure was never to be formed.

Victor Hawley and Mary Jones did not return to that enclosure; they did have children; but they and not their betters made those decisions. Hawley and Jones joined the race, joined the crowd, merged themselves (at least for awhile) with the common course of humanity, producing five children; Bertha and Berton (twins), born in 1879; Romeo, 1880; Rollin, 1882; Corinna, 1885. The twins were born on February 21, 1879. The day before—February 20—was always celebrated at Oneida as "the high tide of the spirit," in contrast to August 20 the "high tide of the flesh." In the case of Victor Hawley and Mary Jones it was a day when both the flesh and the spirit were at their high tide.

Victor Hawley died at Baldwinsville on June 2, 1893 of pneumonia. According to a death announcement he was survived by a wife and three children. Mary Jones moved to California in 1903, and the last notice of her before her death in 1906 comes from a letter of Alfred Hawley to William Hinds in March 1904. Hinds had apparently sent on twenty dollars for use by a community member, and Alfred had finally used it. "When Mary Hawley came here to Los Angeles we had great difficulty in finding her. Burton would not tell Arline (Alfred's daughter) whom he met frequently in Los Angeles-Mrs.Hawley and I went to Los Angeles on purpose to see her, but failed to find her." Later, however, Emerson Marks, Martha Hawley's son, did locate her, and "he found her living in a barn in poverty." A trunk pawned by her son (who drank and gambled) was retrieved, and money was given for her board. Mary's prospects—she was then 62—were not good because only a little money was available to her from some California property, and her son was unreliable. But Alfred saw a bright spot in what must have been a desperate time. "Mary is able to be out with the baby (her grandaughter Helen) in the carriage. So she is much better. We are in hope that they will make a go of it."

Neither Victor Hawley nor Mary Jones are buried at the cemetery at Oneida.

Bibliographic Sources
Index

Bibliographic Sources

𝒲ith the transfer of extant Oneida Community documents to Syracuse University in 1982 and the subsequent opening of those documents in 1991 a new era in the interpretive history of Oneida began. Before 1991 scholars had to rely on a limited body of primary sources published by descendants, printed materials culled (often by descendants) from an enormous body of sermons, commentaries, and periodicals. Contradictory rumors were rife in the scholarly world that a large cache of documents actually existed, or that it had been burned by descendants in an effort to protect reputations and sanitize the history. Now we know that not only had material been burned, that efforts had been made to keep the record free of blemish, but also, surprisingly, that an enormous volume of both personal and documentary evidence had been saved by other descendants.

Before 1991 researchers always began by looking at Robert Allerton Parker's *A Yankee Saint: John Humphrey Noyes and the Oneida Community* (New York, 1935) and George Wallingford Noyes, ed., *The Religious Experience of John Humphrey Noyes* (New York, 1923). These were basic mines of information by a community descendant and a historian who had gained both access to and the confidence of key family members. These sources provided enough materials for commentators from Vernon Louis Parrington in *Main Currents in American Thought* (New York, 1927) to Alice Felt Tyler in *Freedom's Ferment* (Minneapolis, 1934) to weave contradictory views of Noyes as a tyrant or as a benevolent leader, and of the community as a progressive haven or as a den of iniquity.

With the publication of a comprehensive guide to *The Oneida Community Collection in the Syracuse University Library* (Syracuse, 1961) ("the largest group of Oneida Community historical materials outside of private ownership") by Lester Wells, researchers such as myself gained access to a full run of the colony's periodical literature and a substantial body of printed sources. That collection not only deepened our understanding of the social sources of the society, but provided insight into business affairs, relations with other reformers, and a sharper public view of the society. There was still much reading between the lines, ferreting out of data, and continuous interpretation of Oneida's place in reform history. It was not until the publication of Maren Lockwood Carden's *Oneida: Utopian Community to Modern Corporation* (Baltimore, 1969) that "new" material emerged that threw considerable light on the sexual life at Oneida. Carden had been able to gain access to certain private papers but was circumspect about revealing sources and did not emphasize internal struggles and Noyes's dominant role.

As more primary sources emerged, such as Constance Noyes Robertson's bowdlerized two-volume documentary history, in the early 1970s, the scholarly analyses grew more sophisticated. In one year, two books (each with extensive bibliographies) that compared the Oneida Community, the Shakers, and the Mormons appeared, Louis Kern's *Ordered Love* (Chapel Hill, 1981), which made use of material at the Kinsey Institute and focused on the domination of women at Oneida, and Lawrence Foster's *Religion and Sexuality* (New York, 1981), which provided a close reading of religious texts and tensions. In different ways, both Foster and Kern opened up comparative approaches and forced scholars to take a closer look at both their assumptions about Oneida and the details of its history.

Another hint that there was a whole other body of source material came in 1988 with the publication in the journal *Communal Studies* (vol. 8) of "The Status and Self-Perception of Women in the Oneida Community," by Ellen Wayland-

Smith, another descendant and at that time an undergraduate at Amherst College. Using a thesis derived from Carol Gilligan's *In A Different Voice* on gender identity and hitherto unpublished diary material, Wayland-Smith tried to modify Kern's work by examining the different expectations that men and women had at Oneida. By the early 1990s it was apparent that the private sources had been seen by descendants and others, that there was an enormous body of periodical and documentary evidence, and that the combined materials would force a new interpretation of John H. Noyes and the Oneida Community.

Within a year of the opening of the complete collection at Syracuse, Spencer Klaw published his *Without Sin: The Life and Death of the Oneida Community* (New York, 1992). Klaw had been at work on the book since the 1970s, and he had had access to the diary sources while they were in private hands. His work contains new information, though there is no new interpretation, and he failed to digest that enormous body of sources (seventy-five manuscript boxes) and to provide a substantial historical context.

The sources that went into my own analyses were drawn from the forty-year run of the periodical journals (from *The Perfectionist* [1834] to *American Socialist* [1879]) and from articles I published in the *New England Quarterly* and *Labor History* based on them; from Noyes's own writings to new "Home Talks" in the Syracuse Collection; from scientific journals (including animal husbandry tracts at the British Museum); and from a vast array of scholarly monographs on sexual behavior and the history of Oneida (including an edition of *The Daily Journal* I edited in 1975). The original diary came into my possession in 1980 and I worked on it intermittently over the next ten years.

When the "new" material opened at Oneida, I read the diaries cited by Wayland-Smith and the diary of Tirzah Miller used extensively (and selectively) by Spencer Klaw, but I chose to keep my focus on Victor Hawley's account because of its unique nature and because of the dramatic "story" embedded in its pages. Charlotte Leonard's diary, for example, briefly touches on events in 1870 before focusing on events of the crucial year of 1876. Jane Kinsley's "Family History" (written in 1914) downplays the destructive character of complex marriage and offers a child's-eye view. The "new" collection contains a number of "Hawley Family" letters that serve to complement material found in the Nash Papers at Stanford. Beyond those primary resources, I have explored the vast literature of the "diary," using Thomas Mallon's *A Book of One's Own* (New York, 1984) as a primary guide. Throughout this book I have kept the scholarly apparatus to a minimum and tried to focus on both the personal and the intimate qualities of the love that Mary Jones and Victor Hawley had for one another without distorting its place within the larger history of the Oneida Community.

Index

Italic page number denotes illustration.

Utopianism and Communitarianism
Lyman Tower Sargent and Gregory Claeys, *Series Editors*

This series offers historical and contemporary analyses of utopian literature, communal studies, utopian social theory, broad themes such as the treatment of women in these traditions, and new editions of fictional works of lasting value for both a general and scholarly audience.